RESPECTFULLY AND AFFECTIONATELY
DEDICATED TO

TERESIO BOSCO

AND

MARTIN McPAKE

Salesians very near to the heart of
Saint John Bosco.

SALESIAN COLLEGE FARNBOROUGH

Presented to

Jack Heath
7 St Aidan's

on joining
the Salesian family
September 2012

Fr Patrick Sherlock SDB
College Chaplain

SAINT JOHN BOSCO
the priest, the man, the times

by William R. Ainsworth, SDB

SECOND EDITION

ISBN 0 85244 149 5

Printed by:
ALPHA PRINTING, HOLLINWOOD, OLDHAM

Contents

Contents cont'd.

Foreword

IN 1979, THE Salesians in Italy published 'a new biography' of Saint John Bosco by Father Teresio Bosco, SDB, possibly the best of the many such books published on the Saint in the hundred years since his death in January 1888.

The official MEMORIE BIOGRAFICHE of his life consist of twenty large volumes, of which the twentieth contains only the index to the others in 600 pages! No wonder Father Teresio laments having to squeeze his entire work into some 450 pages!

The present modest little work squeezes the life of this remarkable Saint into little more than a third of Father Teresio's and is meant as an introduction to 'Don Bosco' for those who may not have met him before. But in the hundred years since his death there have obviously been new insights, new angles on his life and times, new stories from those who lived and worked with him; for instance, a mature woman, born blind and cured as a child by Our Lady at the intercession of Don Bosco, comes back to tell us, thirty years after his death, that her sight is still perfect. I am quite confident that even those who already love Don Bosco will find much that is new in this little book.

On the occasion of the centenary of the Saint's death, I decided to produce a short work based very loosely on Father Teresio's book. It is by no means a straight resumé: some chapters come directly from the MEMORIE, others embody articles I had written for the SALESIAN BULLETIN over many years. But nevertheless, I freely acknowledge my debt to Father Teresio perhaps especially with regard to the complicated politics of 19th century Italy. Of Father Teresio's considerable detail, given for Italians, I have used only the minimal background essential to the framework of Don Bosco's life; but thanks largely to Don Teresio, one can vouch for its accuracy. Should there be faults, they must be entirely mine.

After all this, the least I can do is to dedicate this little book to Father Teresio Bosco and with him to a dear friend and colleague of his and mine, Father Martin McPake, until his recent death the Regional Superior of world-wide English speaking Salesians, two great sons of Don Bosco who so truly reflect his spirit, his charisms, his love for mankind and especially for the youth of that mankind in all its needs and problems.

W. R. Ainsworth, SDB

Chapter One
TURKEYS

JOHNNY AND JOE were feeling important. Mother had given them the job of watching the turkeys, seeing that they didn't stray and that no-one picked one up. Johnny was five and Joe all of seven. They looked with suspicion at the tall man who smiled at them across the hedge. He came in as he spoke. "Couple of good lads you two, doing a job for your Mum, eh? You want to look out for thieves. But I'm not a thief. I want to buy one of your turkeys and I'll give you a good price for it, too. Five whole soldi! How's that, eh?"

To little country boys who rarely ever saw any money, let alone five whole soldi, this was riches indeed. The man solemnly counted out the money, popped the heaviest turkey in his bag and made off. The two heroes abandoned the rest of them and rushed off to the farmhouse, "Mamma, Mamma, we've sold a turkey and got a jolly good price for it, too! Five soldi". Poor Mamma. "But look, Mamma, five whole soldi!" "Oh you silly boys! Our turkeys are worth four and a half lire each in the market!" (A lira was worth twenty soldi.) "That man was a thief!"

Young Johnny Bosco took that lesson hard. It was some time later when he was by himself watching the turkeys that he noticed a man strolling through the field somewhat away from him. He counted the birds, once, twice, yes, there was one missing! He rushed out into the lane after the man, shouting,

"Hey, mister! You've taken one of our turkeys!"

"Taken one of your turkeys? Well, well, well, what a little joker we have here! If I've taken one of your turkeys, where is it? I'm a clever man I know, but even I can't put a big turkey up my sleeve!" and he opened his arms wide.

"I don't care, you've taken one and I want it back! If you don't give it to me, I'll run after you wherever you go, all day if you like, and I'll yell, 'Thief, thief!' and I'll never stop!" Which he proceeded to do until at last the man, to shut him up said it was all a little joke he was playing on him and showed him where he had hidden the bird in a bag under a hedge. He would, of course, have come back after dark to retrieve it.

Johnny told the proud tale to his mother but she was not too happy about it. "That man could have beaten you and hurt you. I'd sooner have let the turkey go." But Johnny felt better now about losing the first one. He was David against the giant Goliath his mother had told him about and he had won and he wasn't going to be afraid ever as long as he was in the right. As long as he felt he was in the right, he would face any odds. All his life, he would. And did.

Chapter Two
TRAGEDY, FAMILY AND NATIONAL

THE ODDS AGAINST John (Giovanni) Bosco started from his infancy. His father, Francesco, widowed with one son, Anthony, married Margaret Occhiena to whom were born two sons, Joseph (Giuseppe) in 1813, John on August 16th, 1815. He was a small farmer, who, when possible, would help a neighbour, to earn a few extra lire for the family budget. Tragically he caught a chill when he was only thirty-three and died of pneumonia. His mother was already living with them so Margaret had to cope alone with five mouths to feed. She was twenty-nine but had no thought of remarriage. She could be said to be illiterate but had the wisdom of grace and experience; she was strong, energetic and eminently practical, the acknowledged mistress at the Becchi, the Bosco farm area.

John was two when his father died but remembered clearly the hard winter that followed, in 1817. No doubt his mother had later filled in the details. The autumn crops had everywhere failed, famine threatened, and even the stocks built up by thrifty small farmers finally disappeared. Margaret, in a crisis, gave what money she had to a neighbour to buy food at any price; he came back empty-handed and wide-eyed with fear for his own family. Margaret showed her mettle. "We have not eaten this day and eat we must. Come and help me kill the last calf." It represented their last available capital. No matter; they killed it and she gave a substantial portion to the neighbour for his own family. The family ate that night. With the utmost care they survived, even scouring the fields and woods for edible wild plants. The depredations of marauding armies had sharpened the knowledge of these things among the peasantry over generations.

National Tragedy

John was born in the year of Napoleon's final defeat: 1815, but his tyrannical shadow had darkened the sunny Italian skies for a long decade of years, at least for the womenfolk. For the men, perhaps, it was different. The French military genius had swept all Italy into his net and such was the glory of his triumphant 'revolutionary' army that tens of thousands of Italians obeyed willingly his call to arms under the imperial colours. But 20,000 had not returned from Spain and Portugal against Wellington; and 25,000 more perished in the bitter cold of the 1812 retreat from Moscow. Thousands more crept back, crippled and maimed, to their mothers, their wives and children, to their grieving womenfolk who were constrained to sing every Sunday at Mass, "Domine, salvum fac imperatorem nostrum Napoleonem," God save our Emperor Napoleon!

The Emperor had made all Italy one. The subsequent Council of Vienna of 1815 ended that. Italy was again divided into eight slices like a pie; all the kinglets returned, each independent, as did the Papal States, resuming their independence under the Pope. Italy, as a nation, became once again 'a geographical expression'. But the revolutionary virus had taken deep root. All these petty kingdoms, with their separate tariffs and passports, were an affliction upon the people who had recently been one nation, even under a tyrant. For the next fifty years John Bosco lived in an atmosphere of constant political disorder. One by one the kinglets disappeared until at last the Papal States alone stood against the cry of 'one land, one nation, one people'. In 1870, they too succumbed, a tale we shall in due course unfold.

Chapter Three
THE FIRST DREAM

BY THE TIME he was nine, young Johnny was already doing his share of the multiple jobs of the farm, such as hoeing and weeding, watching the stock as, of course, he had been doing as a small child. But John's mother would see that he had his time for play. His strength and inventive mind made him something of a leader even at that age; sometimes, of course, he would be challenged and would come home with a black eye and bleeding nose. "I don't like you playing with those rough boys," Margaret objected as she patched him up. "You should keep away."

"But, Mamma we're not fighting all the time and anyway, when I'm with them, we don't have those bad words you don't let us say, because I won't have them either."

One night, asleep on his straw mattress in the attic, he dreamt he was with a crowd of boys who began to fight and use foul language. John yelled at them to no avail and finally waded in with fists flying. Let him tell the story himself.

"At that moment, I heard someone speaking to me. 'You won't win these boys over with your fists, John. Only with gentleness will they respond. You must learn to help them to see how ugly sin is and how precious is virtue.' At once there was silence and all the boys gathered round the speaker. I saw a man, of noble appearance, whose presence overawed me, but I faced up to him and said, 'Who are you to tell me to do these impossible things?'

'They seem impossible to you now but with obedience and knowledge they won't be.'

'And how am I to get this knowledge?'

'I shall give you a Mistress who will teach you.'

'But sir, who are you?'

'I am the son of her whom your mother has taught you to salute three times a day. Ask my Mother for my name.'

'Then I saw at his side a Lady of majestic appearance whose dress shone like the sun. She beckoned me to come nearer and took my hand.

'Look,' she said. I looked and saw all the boys had turned into animals, goats, dogs, cats, sheep, bears and others.

'Here is your field of work. Make yourself humble, strong, and robust. And what in a moment you will see happen to these animals, you will do for my children' and then I saw all the animals become lambs, playing and frollicking around the Lady and the Man. But it was all too much for me and I began to cry. The Lady put her hand kindly on my head and said, 'At the right time, you will understand'. Then there was a noise and I woke up. In the morning I told my brothers and they burst out laughing. 'Perhaps you'll become a shepherd,' said Joseph. 'More likely a robber chief!' thought Anthony. Mamma said quietly, 'Perhaps it means you might be a priest one day.' But Grandmother said, 'You shouldn't take any notice of dreams at all'. That settled it and I agreed with her but I couldn't get that dream out of my mind."

Margaret, like another mother, kept these things in her heart and there is no doubt that in that heart a seed was sown.

In 1822, the Piedmont government announced a programme of free, compulsory elementary education for all. It took time to implement and in country areas was no more than basic. Shortly after the dream, the nine year old John was able to go to the village school in the November of 1824. The course was to give the three R's, adding a fourth one, religion. It lasted for the farmers' boys through what they called the 'dead season,' when nothing much could be done in the fields. On March 31st it ended and John came away. But he had learned to read and from then on books became a passion for him, especially during the dark nights.

Margaret had never been to school at all but she had a retentive memory and used the long winter nights to give to the three boys the catechism as she had learnt it by heart at Sunday school. She taught them their prayers, the three times a day Angelus, the rosary, she explaind the great feasts of the Church and the seasons, the Ten Commandments and those of the Church, as far as they were able to understand. The Sunday Masses and sermons added to their knowledge and she would qurestion them on what they had heard and understood. There was grace before and after every meal and family prayers at night. The boys made their first confessions long before they were admitted to Holy Communion; on Saturdays she would go with them, make her own confession and after they had made theirs, help them with their thanksgiving. The usual age for first Communion was twelve but when Margaret took John to the curate when he was eleven, the priest was satisfied that he knew his catechism and accordingly admitted him to receive the sacrament.

Chapter Four

THE WORST WINTER

THE JOY OF John's first Holy Communion flowed over into an awareness of the abiding presence of God and the budding of an apostolate. John had unusual physical strength and an equally unusual memory; he was also sharp-eyed, patient and tenacious. Work there was aplenty for an eleven year old but there were the Sundays and the holy days of obligation free except for Mass and the feeding of animals. John built up on his gifts of leadership by embarking on a scheme of entertainment, for young and old. Entertainments were few indeed in the rural areas and were usually confined to individual conjurors and jugglers who would attract curious crowds in village squares. John watched them with intense concentration and then went home to experiment. In later years he marvelled himself at his success. "By the time I was eleven I could perform any trick of conjuring or juggling that I had ever seen; at the cost of many a fall and many a bruise, I could even walk the tightrope on my mother's clothesline."

The locals flocked to the Becchi for the free Sunday evening show. Free in money but there was an obligation. Halfway through the performance John would stop the show. "Now, we'll have a break; we'll say a décade of the rosary or the litany of Our Lady" if it was one of her feasts. Sometimes with complete assurance, John would go through the morning's sermon, "in case some of you weren't there or went to sleep". Not all welcomed this interlude and would move off. "All right, you can go; but don't you come back for the second half!"

Margaret would watch him now and then in wonder. One day she turned to a neighbour, "What do you think of my boy? What do you think he will become?" "I don't know but he'll certainly be up to some devilment somewhere!" It was said with a smile but nevertheless there was a shade of fear as these highly superstitious country folk watched the conjuring tricks they could not understand. Occasionally, John could see his brother Anthony standing at the back and heard his remark. "Oh, yes, quite the little entertainer, enjoying himself while the rest of us break our bones with work."

Anthony was becoming a problem. That year, the grandmother, his father's mother, died and he felt increasingly isolated. He incessantly grumbled to Margaret that the heaviest burden of the work fell upon him while John, in particular, got all the attention. She would reply patiently that both John and Joseph did their full share of the work of the farm and only at night did John turn to his books. Books were rare in any farmhouse but he had been able to borrow a couple. Unhappily the very sight of a book served to infuriate Anthony.

"What do we want books for? They don't make you strong for work. I'm as strong as anyone and I've never bothered with books!"

John would answer back. "Oh yes, our old donkey is as strong as you and it can't read either!" Sometimes he managed to get out of range but sometimes he could not and had to cry himself to sleep with swollen eyes and bruised cheeks. In tears, too, was Margaret lying awake in her lonely bed. The winter passed in misery, the 'worst winter of my life' as John later described it. On a bitter February day, matters came to a head.

Anthony came in from the yard and found John reading at the kitchen table. He snatched the book from him and pitched it into the fire. John raced to rescue it before much damage had been done. But this was the end.

Anthony stormed at them. "I'll not have anyone reading when I come in; from now on I am going to throw every book I see into the fire; and that's final!"

Nothing Margaret could say made any difference. She went up to John's room with him.

"We can't carry on like this, son. I'm sorry but there is only one thing to do. Tomorrow you must leave home."

Chapter Five

BREAD, WORK AND PEACE

"BUT MAMMA! OH Mamma! Leave home? Where can I go?"

"I'll pack you up something in the morning and you can follow the road to Moncucco. There are several farms on that road who know me. One of them might give you a job for a while. Then if you go through the village there are cousins of ours, the Moglias. If you haven't got in anywhere, go to them. Ask for Signor Luigi." And in the morning she made up a pack of the few clothes the boy possessed, his precious couple of books, some bread. There was snow on the road and a heavy mist as she gave him a final hug and sent him off, watching him and waving to him until she could no longer see him in the frosty haze. She went back to her kitchen, grieving and praying with all the mothers of the world who have had to send their sons away, to work or to war.

The boy trudged away with death in his heart, a shocked, bewildered lad still six months from his twelfth birthday.

At each of the farms his mother mentioned he was turned away. It was still the 'dead season' and there was no work for anyone. So, in the late afternoon, his bread and his hopes all gone, he asked the way to the Moglia farm. As he turned in at the gate an old man was about to bar it.

"What are you looking for, boy?"

"Work."

"Good. Work away. Goodbye," and he lifted the heavy bar again.

"But I must see Signor Luigi."

The Moglia family were in the portico, working on something for the vineyard.

"I'm looking for Signor Luigi."

"You are speaking to him."

"My mother sent me. She told me to come to you to ask for a job as a stable boy."

"But surely she hasn't sent a little fellow like you away from home? Who is your mother?"

"Margaret Bosco. My brother Anthony beats me so mother told me to come to you to ask for a job."

"But, my poor boy, it's winter. We don't take anybody until the end of March. Listen, son, the best thing you can do is to have patience and go back home."

All John's courage and vaunted bravado vanished; like any other cold, frightened, exhausted child, he burst into tears.

"Please, please, let me come. I can't go back, I can't! I'll work for nothing, as long as you like, if you'll only let me stay!"

Luigi's wife, Dorothy, herself only twenty-five, tried to comfort him.

"Take him, Luigi, just to try him out for a few days."

Teresa, who was fifteen and Luigi's little sister, also felt sorry for him. "Look, Luigi, I'm old enough to work with you in the fields now. The boy could easily do my job in the stable."

So it was done. John began work as a stable boy in February 1827 and remained with the Moglias for nearly three years, beyond all his hopes.

They were well-to-do farmers, even though the whole family worked from dawn to dusk. They were also a model family in other ways. Every night there were family prayers and soon John was asked to take his turn in leading the rosary. On Sundays Luigi drove the whole family to the 'grand Mass' in Moncucco, at which in those days the entire village was present.

It was not long before Luigi remarked to his wife, "You know, Dorothy, we did no bad thing in giving that lad a job; he's a grand little worker!"

Shortly after his arrival, John asked, at the Saturday evening supper, for permission to go to Moncucco early the following morning. This happened each Saturday. Dorothy, who felt that she was in his mother's place, was curious to know what he was doing. She got up with the dawn one Sunday and from the house of a friend in Moncucco saw John arrive and go into the church. She followed him in, saw him go to confession and receive Holy Communion at the Mass, the 'low Mass'. In those somewhat Jansenistic days it was rare for anyone to go to weekly communion and it was not distributed at all at the 'high Mass'. Dorothy met John on the way out and they walked back together for breakfast after which John as always went with the family to the principal Mass. Dorothy said to him, "In future, John, you can go to the early Mass whenever you want and there's no need to ask permission".

She gave him a small but pleasant room to himself; in every way, he was far better off than he had been at home. He used to read by candlelight at night and no-one objected. He would go to confession to Don Cottino, the parish priest, to whom he confided his strong desire to become a priest and all the difficulties that seemed to make that impossible. The priest encouraged him to keep up his courage and his prayers, have patience and trust God to make His will known. Now and again he would give him some help with basic Latin and lend him a few books.

His friendship with the parish priest led him to friendship with the village children. On Sunday afternoons, and on the major feast days, he would gather them together in the school, make them laugh with his tricks, read them Old Testament stories, lead them in simple prayers. When the hard winter weather made it impossible to go to Moncucco, some children from nearby farms would make their way to the Moglias and he would collect them together in the barn, play with them and give them catechism lessons. It was the germ of his future 'festive oratory'.

He was happy at the Moglias, regretting only the passing of years, leaving him no further in essential studies. Yet they were not wasted years. His farm work, often allowing him to work alone, helped him to keep in the presence of God, to deepen his awareness of God and to learn the essentials of contemplation, possibly without being aware of it. There is no doubt that the peaceful years on the Moglia farm were fruitful for his spiritual life and progress.

His absence from his mother was a constant pain for Margaret. In November 1829, she could stand it no longer. Anthony was now twenty-one and thinking of getting married. Somehow John must be allowed to study. She asked her brother, his Uncle Michael, to see John and bring him home. John said an emotional farewell to his friends whom he remembered all his life with gratitude and deep affection. There was tension when he arrived at the Becchi but not war. As long as Anthony was assured that he would not have to contribute to his brother's studies, he was satisfied. The question now was how to start the studies, and where; John was now fourteen and really too big for primary education. A quite unforeseen happening seemed to present a perfect solution.

Chapter Six
IN THE CANONRY

IN THAT YEAR of 1829, a venerable old priest, Don Giovanni Calosso, took over the nearby parish of Murialdo, having in view of his failing health relinquished a much larger parish some distance away. In the November of John's return from the Moglias, there was a mission in another local parish which John attended. On the way back, walking alone, he overtook the old priest making his slow way home.

"Ah, young man, where have you been?"

"I've been to the mission, Father."

"So have I, my son; but surely you wouldn't have understood much of that sermon with all its Latin quotations?"

"Oh," replied John, "I think I managed fairly well to understand it all."

"All? Look, I'll give you four soldi if you can tell me four words of it!"

"Certainly, Father," and John proceeded to go through the entire sermon as they walked along, to the stupefaction of Don Calosso. He wanted to know John's name, heard of his hopes for the priesthood, his frustrations and problems. Before they parted, he asked John to tell his mother that he would like to see her. She went up the next day.

"Look, Signora, your son has a prodigious memory and simply must be helped with his studies. If you'll let him come to me, I'll do all I can to help him."

It was arranged that John would go over to him for Latin lessons every day, returning home to sleep. In times of urgent work on the farm, he would take his share but otherwise his time was spent in the company of Don Calosso in the canonry. It was a wonderful year of progress in every way. They would go through the scriptures and John was encouraged to make a simple meditation each day. In the September of 1830, he moved over entirely to the canonry, repaying the old priest with whatever services he could perform.

"I loved him as a father," wrote John later, "I opened my heart to him and let him guide me in all I did. He returned my affection and gave me as much time as he could spare in correcting my work and instructing me in the spiritual life." It was a time of the greatest consolation to both John and

Margaret, for more than once Don Calosso declared that as long as he lived he would see John right through his studies for the priesthood, and if he died, well, he had thought of that, too. It all seemed too good to last.

Just a year after that fortuitous meeting, in November, John happened to be at home when an urgent message sent him flying back to Murialdo. He found Don Calosso collapsed in a chair, unable to speak, suffering from a severe stroke. He managed to indicate to John where the key of his bureau was and by signs to show that whatever was in it, was for him, for his studies. Shortly afterwards, to John's inconsolable grief, he died. The bureau contained some 6,000 lire, not a fortune but quite ample to finance all John's studies right up to the priesthood.

However, when the family arrived for the funeral and enquired about what Don Calosso had left, John simply handed them the key of the bureau. They were well aware of the old priest's intentions and invited John to take whatever he needed of the money. But he felt he could not and returned to the Becchi. With Don Calosso's death had died all his hopes, and now, at fifteen, he had no teacher, no money and no plans for the future.

Musical Tailor

John, however, had still to learn that God has plans. To clear the way, Margaret decided that the little family patrimony be divided according to the law, Anthony taking his share on the occasion of his marriage and be thus independent of the family. Margaret and Joseph ran their part of the farm and took on other work, while she decided that John should attend the local school at Castelnuovo d'Asti, a small town some five kilometres away, where a Latin class had been added to the school course. Uncle Michael fixed up a 'semipension' with a Signor Roberto; John could sleep there and would receive 'soup' for lunch and supper, while Margaret would provide bread and pay the modest pension, usually in kind, from the produce of the farm.

The school soon turned out to be a waste of time as well as an embarrassment for John. At fifteen he had to sit with boys of ten or eleven who laughed at him as 'the big country yokel with clothes stolen from a scarecrow!' A weak teacher, trying to curry favour with the class he could not control, joined in the derision, refused to correct John's work as beneath his dignity and made it impossible for him to make any progress. Poor John. After the bliss of the canonry and Don Calosso, it was a 'via crucis,' indeed. Given a chance he could have exercised all his old mastery with these boys but no chance was ever given. Margaret decided that he should leave and prepare to go to the secondary school in the provincial town of Chieri, for the school year of 1831. Meanwhile, he had to get through this year. There were compensations.

Signor Roberto was the town's leading tailor and in the long evenings John was eager to help; he soon picked up the essentials and indeed made such good progress that Signor Roberto offered him a permanent job. But the good tailor was also the leading musician and parish organist and again John responded with enthusiasm to his invitation to pick up music. He was soon showing promise on the Signor's spinet and on the church organ; later he acquired a fiddle and could produce a tolerable tune on that.

That was not all. When he left school and during the wait for the move to Chieri, John, with the agreement of his mother, got a job for some hours each day with the local blacksmith. Quite apart from the forge he learnt to use simple engineering tools. With his eye on the priesthood, he probably thought that all these extraneous activities were just a waste of time. In fact, he was laying foundations. Everything he learnt at Castelnuovo d'Asti was to prove of inestimable value to him in later years his music, his tailoring, the use of the tools at the blacksmith's. And just about that time, he had that dream again; the noble Lady, the quarrelling boys who turned into lambs, under his care.

Chapter Seven

GREEN YEARS AT CHIERI

CHIERI WAS, AND still is, a pleasant, busy town about eight miles from Turin, the capital city of Piedmont. When John Bosco arrived there, in the St. Martin's summer of November 1831, it held about 9,000 inhabitants, the majority of them getting their living as silk and cotton weavers in one of the thirty establishments of the town; it was also a 'city of convents, monasteries and students'. In addition to the schools, many religious orders, the Dominicans, Redemptorists, Jesuits and Franciscans also had their seminaries there for their own clerical students.

John wrote, "I was boarding in the house of Lucia Matta, a widow with one only son, who had moved there to look after him as he attended school". Margaret arrived just after John, bringing with her on a neighbour's cart two bags of grain, as part payment of the 'pension'. "I'll do all I can to keep up the payments, in cash or in kind, and my son will play his part, you may be sure."

At school, John was again somewhat of a 'pillar' among the younger boys, but he found his priest teachers sympathetic and well satisfied with his obvious intelligence and remarkable memory. He soon moved up the school, leapfrogging some of the earlier classes. It took a little time to find his place among these, generally better off, students, country lad as he was, but soon his scholastic progress won for him their admiration. They began to turn to him for help and he would pass on to any who asked him for his quickly finished work for them to copy. This was ere long discovered by the masters and he was duly reprimanded, though in kindly fashion, as he was becoming a star pupil and usually top of the class at the end of the term. Though rightly forbidden to pass on his finished work, he was always ready to help out with difficult problems.

His mother would come along every now and then bringing what she could to Lucia and happy to hear that good lady's encomiums of her son. John did his best to encourage Lucia's rather lazy son to work harder and was also ready to help in the house in any way he could. During school holidays he found a part-time job with a carpenter and joiner, thus adding to his 'trades' some knowledge of simple building and getting to know the woodworking tools, all grist to the mill he had not yet dreamed of.

Meanwhile he had to learn to meet life in some of its less pleasing forms. The religious atmosphere at the school was extremely strict by modern standards but some students reacted against it. They took advantage of John's easy approach to try to involve him in some of their questionable activities, in which robbing his mother or his landlady was about the mildest.

"You have to learn to live, man, and you can't live without money. If they won't give you any, you must get some . . ."

He was old enough to look after himself but realised that many of the younger boys, some fresh from the country, would easily give way to pressure of this sort. He got together a few of the better disposed boys and started what he called the 'Societa dell'Allegria'. 'Allegria' means joy, happiness, cheerfulness. He proposed three simple rules:

1. No act or word that could make any decent Catholic ashamed.
2. To carry out one's duties, scholastic and religous.
3. To be cheerful . . . 'allegro'. (Musically minded folk will recognise the word.)

John was soon in his element gathering around him an enthusiastic group whom on occasion he would entertain in the old Becchi fashion, especially in wet weather, with his tricks, gymnastics, juggling and conjuring. As always, the show ended with a prayer. "We used to end up in the church of St. Anne, where the Jesuit Fathers gave us some great talks, telling us things I still remember."

He became famous at school and indeed in the town, when one Sunday he took on a professional entertainer who was drawing large crowds on the Sunday morning at Mass time and challenging all and sundry to beat him. John's friends urged him to take the man on, and put up the first wager of twenty lire for the first encounter. It was a race, in which the professional soon got ahead but tired over the longer distance. The wager was double or quits each time. The man put up his forty lire for the next try, a jumping contest and lost again; also for the third. Finally, there was a juggling act. The man put up a brilliant performance and seemed certain to win at least this one when his rather long nose got in the way of a difficult manoeuvre and the trick collapsed. John and the group felt rather sorry for him and gave him back their now considerable winnings on condition that he stood them a good lunch and agreed not to perform again on the town square during the time of the principal Mass. The conditions were gratefully accepted, the lunch was a good one, and 'allegria' all round was the order of the day . . . . As it was, in general, throughout John's green years at Chieri.

Chapter Eight

THE SEASON OF FRIENDSHIPS

IN THE AUTUMN of 1832 John Bosco began his final two years at Chieri. He was eighteen, the age of friendship. Apart from his little army of followers, there was a close circle of intimate friends some of whom remained so until the end of their lives. One of the early ones was a Jew, Giacomo Levi. In the Piedmont of the time, Jews were second class citizens, with many disadvantages. They had to live in a ghetto while coping with a Gentile world. As an Orthodox Jew, Giacomo was forbidden to do any work on the Sabbath, the Saturday, not even his homework. John settled that problem by doing it for him; but there was much else. Naturally, the friends discussed their respective beliefs. Giacomo became interested in Christianity and eventually, to John's delight, and despite threats and warnings from his family, was baptised; he remained true to his newly adopted faith and his friendship with John Bosco until his death.

Another close friend was Luigi Comollo, a classmate, gentle, reserved, the very opposite of John. Once in the delayed absence of the class master, a free-for-all developed to which Comollo played not the slightest attention, getting on with his work. This annoyed some of the wilder sort and they tried to drag him into the fray, finally resorting to blows. John saw red, and forgetting that dream 'not by blows but by gentleness,' waded in to protect his friend. In fact, lacking any weapon, he picked up one of the attackers and used him as a battering ram to scatter the others. Comollo's comment was, "You frighten me, John. Your great strength was not given you to massacre your companions. As Christians we have to turn the other cheek." John, suitably chastened, went to confession and started again to try to keep that resolution. It was never easy for him. Of Luigi Comollo, we shall have much more to say.

But as the school years ended he began to think hard about his future. A priest, yes, but just how long could he expect his poor mother to find the means? The seminary fees would be beyond her. He thought hard about joining an Order. They would advance him to the priesthood without burdening his mother; in fact, he approached the Franciscans who told him they were prepared even to forego the fees they usually asked from students before profession.

On the other hand, as his parish priest pointed out, as a parish priest he would be able to support his mother in her old age, which he would not be able to do in a monastery. Margaret, however, would have none of this argument. In fact, she told John, that if he ever had the misfortune to become a wealthy priest she would not darken his doors; she wanted nothing from his priesthood. Then John had a dream of an old friar who said to him, "You will not find with us the peace you are looking for". But who bothers about dreams? Someone suggested, "Why not talk to Don Cafasso?" Why not, indeed. Don Giuseppe (Joseph) Cafasso was himself a native of Castelnuovo d'Asti, a young priest still, but talked about for his austere life and his extraordinary discernment.

He listened carefully while John told him of the financial problem and the dilemma. His reply was clear. "Forget about the monastery. Go to the seminary which is your true vocation. As for the means, do not worry. God will provide." John accepted this counsel without hesitation, as he went on doing for many years, as Don Cafasso became his confessor, his spiritual director, his mentor and benefactor, one of the major influences of his life and work.

Chapter Nine
THE SEMINARY

DON CAFASSO WAS, of course, right about God providing. John's new parish priest's support moved two parishioners to settle John's bill for the final school year, and Don Cafasso himself persuaded the Rector of the seminary to grant him a gratuitous first year.

First had to come the clothing, the vesting of the clerical cassock. This took place in the parish church of Castelnuovo d'Asti, before a large and admiring congregation. There were many tears, from those who knew John's, and Margaret's, story; happy tears too, from Margaret herself. It would be six years before she could call her son 'Don Bosco' but the black cassock was the sure sign that he was on the way, the proof of God's approval. For John, of course, it was a happy day but a solemn one. He drew up, in a personal notebook, a list of stern resolutions, such as he deemed essential for a clerical student on the way to the priesthood. His best biographer comments that he did not keep them all since, like the rest of us, he was flesh and blood; but at least they pointed the way.

On October 30th, 1835, John being now twenty, he entered the great gates of the seminary. He joined the long line of clerics who filed into the chapel to the solemn strains of the organ in the 'Veni Creator'; they settled in for the opening retreat.

The course was for six years, two of philosphy and four of theology, as indeed it is today. The Chieri seminary had only been opened since 1829 but it conformed in every way to the iron discipline and inflexible timetable laid down centuries before in the Counter Reformation. The first thing the students had to learn was that the bell was the voice of God and woe betide anyone who did not instantly obey it. The rising would be at 5 a.m., the day long, and truth to say, monotonous in its unvarying pattern. Meals were taken in silence, a reader supposedly keeping the students interested as he read the history of the Church or the lives of the Fathers. Food was simple, rough and at times, sparse; a stern notice reminded all that "We eat to live, not live to eat". Recreation time after lunch helped to ease the tension but only on Thursday afternoons, free of all studies, could John get a real breath of fresh air. His Chieri boys would clamour at the gate to see him and he could spend a happy couple of hours with them; it was the highlight of the week. Not that he was unhappy; he was doing what he had worked and prayed for and it was good indeed. In writing later about his seminary days, he had two adverse remarks. One was that the superiors kept aloof from the students. The sight of one in the courtyard would cause the students to scatter. John resolved that when he was a priest he would change all that; he would be the first to approach the young. The other sadness concerned the indifference of a minority of the students; some did considerable harm to the weaker ones. He was also rather saddened that the rule laid down, in those rather Jansenistic days, Holy Communion only at the low Mass on Sundays. When the students filed in silence into breakfast during the week, it was possible to slip aside and go to the nearby church of St. Philips: one paid for it by foregoing breakfast. John, and some of the more devout students, did this as often as possible.

In John's second year, Luigi Comollo entered and the two at once resumed their close friendship. Though two years younger, Luigi rather led the way in spiritual things. He would pull John away from recreation for a further half-hour in the chapel; at table he would fast, not only rigorously in Lent, but find many a pretext to do so during the year. Often he would merely dip his bread into water at a main meal. There was no-one to moderate his austerities. Truth to say, he ruined his health by them; in later years when Don Bosco was guiding the young Dominic Savio to sanctity, he would not allow him to go too far. But who are we to judge? God must have loved Luigi in his foolishness, born of love and of sorrow for the sins of the world.

Chapter Ten

THEOLOGY: THE RUN UP TO THE PRIESTHOOD

PHILOSOPHY SCHOOLS ENDED on June 24th, John's 'feast day,' that of St. John the Baptist. He walked the twelve kilometres to his brother Joseph's farm, where he was warmly welcomed by the little family, by Mary the wife and Filomena, the baby daughter. Margaret lived there too but often went to help out at other farms.

John tells us in his 'Memorie' that once when he was working in his brother's vineyard, he started a hare. Without thinking he rushed into the house, grabbed his brother's shotgun and set off across fields and vineyards in chase followed by an enthusiastic group. When after five wild kilometres he finally caught up with the poor animal and shot it, he suddenly remembered the second of his fine 'clothing day' resolutions: "I shall refrain in future from all such things as conjuring, acrobatics *and* hunting". Ah, well . . .

Theology classes began on November 3rd, 1837. Theology is the 'science that studies God'. Its chief elements are Dogmatic theology, the study of Christian truth, Moral, the laws governing Christian morality, Scripture, the word of God, Canon Law, the laws of the Church, Church History, the story of Christianity and its development to modern times. There are several subsidiary subjects deemed to develop the priest's maturity and understanding of the world he lives in. Anyone who works through these sometimes difficult courses conscientiously must be considered as a 'professional' in all the modern connotation of the word.

John Bosco was always a ready student inclined to overwork rather than to slack. Apart from the compulsory subjects he filled his remarkable memory with all the riches he could gather from an extensive library. He was reputed to know the entire four Gospels in Greek and Latin by heart, as likewise he did such classics as Dante's 'Divina Commedia'. He was highly intelligent but not, perhaps, brilliant in the sense of being creative or intuitive. His memory made him an accurate and orderly recorder of known facts, as is evident in the popular books he was later to write. Seminary examiners are apt to demand a great deal of memorial accuracy and it is no wonder that year after year John Bosco carried off the major prizes for study. To these, oddly enough in a seminary, were attached substantial financial rewards, which helped to cover his fees in the final years.

The full course of theology at Chieri lasted not four but five years but by special permission of the Archbishop, John was allowed to cover the fourth year course during the final holiday period which he did successfully.

But first there occurred a strange, disturbing event. One day Luigi Comollo remarked to John how little we know for certain as to who was saved, who went to heaven, or not; even for the apparently pious, there was always a doubt. He proposed to John that, the one who might die the first, would find some means of letting the other know whether he was in heaven or not. Foolishly and dangerously, John agreed and they made a pact.

Shortly afterwards, Luigi collapsed and on April 2nd, 1839, with John holding his hand in grief, he died. He was twenty-two. On the night of April 3rd/4th, as all the students were asleep in the dormitory, they were awakened by a terrible noise approaching the room; some described it as like a 'huge wagon, drawn by galloping horses'. As it approached the door, with an ever increasing roar, the students, including John, leapt from their beds in terror. The door burst open with a blinding flash and there was heard the voice of Luigi Comollo crying, "Bosco, Bosco, I am saved!" The noise then died away and the door closed. John was overwhelmed by the experience and took months to recover. "I fell ill," he said, "and was in bed for months, nearly dying myself." It was a grim warning to him and to all of us that we should not attempt to find out what God does not as a rule choose to reveal to us.

However, he recovered, completed his studies and was admitted to the subdiaconate and diaconate. Finally, on June 5th, 1841, he was ordained by Archbishop Fransoni in his private chapel in Turin.

The next day, he said his first Mass in the church of St. Francis of Assisi, assisted by his friend and benefactor, Don Cafasso. It was the greatest day of his life, he said, as it is for every priest. He prayed for and remembered all who had helped him to that day, his wonderful mother, his dear ones, the family dead, his benefactors with a special memento of his dear Don Calosso, who had indeed done so much to put him on the way.

The next day was the feast of Corpus Christi and this Mass he said in his parish church, in the presence of his mother and family, and of all who had followed his progress through the years, remembering him as the boy who could do so many tricks, how he would entertain them, the boy whom they would meet on the hills, with bare feet, and carrying a book.

Now he was 'Don Bosco'. When Margaret that evening was able to get him to herself for a minute, she said, "Now John, you are a priest and near to Our Lord. I haven't read all your books but believe me when I tell you that when you start to say Mass you will start to suffer. You won't know at once but gradually it will dawn on you. All you must do now has to be for the salvation of souls; you must not bother about me at all."

Among the written resolutions he made that day was this one: "The charity and gentleness of St. Francis de Sales shall be my guide in all I do".

Chapter Eleven
THE REAL WORLD

IT SEEMS THAT, at that time, diocesan priests were not, after ordination, automatically appointed to curacies. Don Bosco was offered various posts, as chaplain or tutor and was free to choose. He turned to Don Cafasso who told him not to take any of them. "Come to us at the Convitto, where you'll do some extra study, some pastoral work and find out where your real work lies."

The Convitto, the St. Francis Priests' House, had been set up by the Seminary Rector, D. Guala, as a two-year perfectionist course for forty-five priests; he had recruited Don Cafasso, who again helped Don Bosco about fees. Don Bosco actually stayed three years there taking his share in lecturing but mainly increasing his priestly experience and meeting the real world of his future work.

On December 8th, 1841, when he was about to offer the Mass of the Immaculate Conception in the church of St. Francis of Assisi, there was a commotion in the sacristy. A boy had crept in; seeing him the sacristan told him to serve Don Bosco's Mass. "I can't, I don't know how." "Then what are you doing here, you rascal! Get out, clear off!" and the irate old man began to belabour the boy with the broom. The priest intervened, "What are you doing, Giuseppe?" as the boy fled. "Call him back, he's a friend of mine." With difficulty, the boy was persuaded to return.

"As soon as I've said Mass, we'll have a talk" and after Mass Don Bosco took him off to a quiet corner. He was an orphan, came from the country, was sixteen, had made a first confession but no more, had forgotten even how to make the sign of the cross. His name was Bartholomew Garelli.

"Can you read and write, son?"

"No."

"Can you sing?"

"Sing? No!"

"Can you whistle . . . like this?"

"Oh, yes!" They laughed and were friends.

"Come along on Sunday and bring a few friends; but first let's say a Hail

Mary" and together they went through the little prayer to Our Lady which, forty-five years later, Don Bosco said was the real start of his work. On the Sunday Garelli came, with eight other building apprentices like himself, to meet the "priest who can whistle, too".

Each Sunday, the numbers grew; soon there was some difficulty in finding suitable venues for what was the beginning of Don Bosco's 'Festive Oratories'; Festive, because they took place on Sundays and days when there was no work, holy days of obligation, feast days; and Oratory, because they were a mixture of pray and play. Don Bosco was free to devote the entire Sunday to them. They would gather at an appointed spot and he would lead them off into the country or to some outlying shrine where he would have arranged to say Mass for them, to give them a short talk, a little catechism, hear confessions, even; and then have a full afternoon of noise and bustle and games of all sorts. He would find little prizes, again helped by Don Cafasso, and even bread and fruit for those without. They would finish up in the evening with Benediction, given a final thought, told where to meet the following week and so home, often some of them escorting a weary priest back to his lodgings.

Meanwhile he was meeting a new world, utterly different than that of his simple country existence, where poverty existed but not destitution, where families still lived Christian lives as he and his brothers had lived at the Becchi.

Rural life could no longer support the teeming thousands who flocked into the city for work and lodging. The industrial revolution, begun largely in England, was sweeping through Europe, and Italy was no exception. Ill-paid, if they had any work at all, ill-lodged, many of the innocents from the country soon fell into gangs, driven to crime and degradation. As the Lady had said to him as a small boy, "These are to be your field of work". He was appalled when he realised it fully. For all his strength of mind and body, Don Bosco was deeply sensitive, soon sickened by what he saw.

Made of sterner stuff, surprisingly, was the frail, almost hunchbacked Don Cafasso who, theologian and ascetic though he was, made it his business to go into the prisons and work untiringly with the inmates. He was, of course, met at the start with the usual derision, blasphemies and obscenities, but he persisted, would never give anyone up, ever trying to bring a little Christian love and understanding into a dreadful environment. Eventually he was accepted, and because he would accompany even the worst criminals to the scaffold, became known as 'the apostle of the gallows'.

He would urge Don Bosco to accompany him or take his place, which he would gladly do, but at times it would be more than he could stand.

Chapter Twelve
TWO SAINTS AT A HANGING

Three men hung from three crosses, condemned to a public death in the sight of all who cared to look, to mock or to mourn. Over the head of the centre one was a crudely written sign in three languages, naming the prisoner as, 'King of the Jews'. One of the hanging criminals joined in the mockery. "Look at him! Some king! Some throne! Why can't your majesty get us down from here?" But the other would not have it. "Shut up, you! We're getting what we've been asking for for a long time but this poor fellow hasn't done anything!" Poor deluded king, pity him. "Sir," he said, "remember me when you come into your kingdom". He heard from the suffering man by his side: "I tell you, this day you will be with me in Paradise". Paradise? Paradise? But through the pain and the misery and the despair, there came to that pitying prisoner a sudden lifting of the heart.

BY THE END of the eighteenth and into the nineteenth century capital punishment could still cover crimes which today would scarcely earn more than a couple of months in prison or even, perhaps, a fine. We may joke, "Might as well be hanged for a sheep as for a lamb!" but then, a man could hang for stealing a lamb. Italy was no exception, though the actual laws might differ in one or other of the petty kingdoms. In Piedmont, of which Turin was the capital, hangings were public, a spectacle that drew fascinated crowds. The Church, however she might deplore the crime, had care for the criminal and did what she could to bring Christ's forgiving mercy to all who would accept it.

In 1846 three men were sentenced to death in the Turin courts. Two were father and son. The son, aged about twenty, had been one of Don Bosco's early boys and now asked him to be with him in the days before the hanging. Don Bosco spent many hours with him in the prison, trying to comfort him. On the final day before the sentence was due to be carried out, the boy then begged him to stand by him on the scaffold. Don Bosco, for all his care, was reluctant to make a firm promise for fear he would not be able to stand the strain and thus fail his poor young friend in the very moment of his need. Don Cafasso, however, constrained him to make the effort.

The actual hanging was to be in the large town of Alexandria. Trains in 1846 were primitive and open. The sentence stipulated that the prisoners would be visible to all as the train stopped at every station, where passengers could join it. The two priests were on this 'death' train, which arrived in the evening before the execution. They were at once taken to the prison. In his 'Life' of Don Cafasso, Don Bosco described what happened in some detail.

"Each of the prisoners was in a cell by himself. When I entered, the poor boy flung himself on me, weeping bitterly. There was one guttering candle for light and we sat in front of it. I tried to find words to comfort him. I helped him to make his last confession, to express his sorrow for what he had done." Don Bosco used all his experience, all his love and pity, to console the weeping frightened boy, his own tears not very far away. "See the crucifix; Our Lord was sinless, yet He suffered, suffered for you too. *He* had to die, so He has been through all this before us. Now you have made your confession, you are sorry for all the sins of your life, so you have nothing to fear. Remember what Our Lord said to that thief on the cross beside Him, 'This day, you will be with Me in Paradise'.? Think of Him saying that to you, too." It was never easy to find words to answer the ultimate question "Why must I die?".

About two in the morning, the guards came to take them to the prison chapel. There were just the two of them. Don Bosco said the Mass at which the boy received Holy Communion. There they sat together until daybreak. Shortly afterwards, the governor came in, accompanied by the hangman, who, as was the custom, knelt down to receive the prisoner's pardon. He then put a noose round his neck and bound his hands. As they were lining up at the main doors, there came the boom of the great bell of the Cathedral; it was the signal to all the city, the 'passing bell,' that someone was near death. This was common in Italy, but all his life, Don Bosco could never hear it without recalling that slow, solemn beat on that awful day.

Outside there were three carts, each with two horses. In the first was a local priest with one of the prisoners, in the second Don Bosco and the boy, and Don Cafasso in the third with the boy's father. Leading the slow procession was a group of blackhooded 'Fratelli della Misericordia,' Brothers of Mercy, headed by one of them bearing a tall crucifix. The Brothers began to chant the Psalm 'Miserere,' in Latin, as they walked, repeating it as the solemn beat of the great bell kept time. The crowds were largely silent, at least at the start; many of the women would make the sign of the cross, staring in awe or fear as the sombre procession passed by.

Once the carts stopped, the police and soldiers halting them outside a church. A group of altar boys came out, carrying candles, followed by a priest in cotta and stole, carrying the Blessed Sacrament, with which he blessed each cart from the steps; he then returned.

The crowds thickened and grew noisier, some shouting ribald remarks, others trying to comfort the prisoners. As they turned a corner, Don Bosco saw the gallows, as did the trembling boy by his side. He felt himself growing faint. Don Cafasso, close behind, must have noticed his white-faced distress: he got down and went across to him. "Come, Don Bosco, I'll go in with the boy and you go with the man; it will be easier for you."

The third cart became separated from the others as the crowd surged around the gallows. Nothing the police or the driver could do could clear the way. The prisoner in the cart, seemingly indifferent to his fate, was amused at their futile efforts. "Hey, you people! What's the hurry? I'm the number one attraction on this show and if you won't let us through, you won't get your money's worth!" Eventually they moved in as the other carts pulled away. There was a roll of drums. Don Bosco, feeling faint and holding on to the side of the cart, looked up and saw his young friend already hanging. As the man with him got down from the cart and began to climb the steps of the scaffold, he remembered no more. When he came to, he was being comforted by Don Cafasso. When he had somewhat recovered, they followed the three coffins to the church of the Brothers and assisted at the Requiem Mass offered at once by the prison chaplain. Thus does the Church show her compassionate concern for all her children even for those who may be no credit to her.

Don Bosco never again attended a public hanging nor did Don Cafasso press him to do so although, until public hangings were abolished, the Turin gallows were only a few hundred yards from the Valdocco house.

Chapter Thirteen

IF I HAD ONLY ONE PIECE OF BREAD, I'D SHARE IT WITH YOU!

IN RELATING THE execution experience, we have rather jumped a little from the early days of Don Bosco's more general work for 'poor and abandoned youth'. His contacts with Garelli and his friends grew rapidly as more and more of them found somewhere good to go to on Sundays and holidays.

One Sunday he was going through the parish church at the time of High Mass during which a young priest was giving a long and erudite sermon, when he noticed a group of boys fast asleep in one of the side altars. He thought he might wake them up which he did with a gentle shake and a smile.

"We couldn't understand that priest's words, Father," they explained a little shamefacedly.

"Come along with me, then, and meet a few more friends," and so saying he took them through the sacristy where Garelli and half a dozen others were already waiting for him. In due time, he said Mass for them and used it to give them some simple basic principles, and a story or two, to help them cope with the difficulties of their lives.

Most of these boys were builders' apprentices, many of them far from their homes. Some of them kept close to Don Bosco all their lives. Amongst the sleepy-heads was one Carlo Buzzetti. In the spring of 1842, he brought his younger brother Giuseppe (Joseph), all of ten years of age (and already a builders' apprentice!) to see Don Bosco and join the group. For the rest of his life Giuseppe stuck to Don Bosco like a limpet. He was never far away from him at any time, shared all the vicissitudes of the early years, became a Brother and was at Don Bosco's bedside when he died, forty-six years later. When there might be some doubts as to this or that happening, Brother Giuseppe's memory could always be relied upon to provide confirmation.

Italian children in those days were always very pleased to receive medals and pictures from the priests, but Don Bosco soon realised that his ever growing troops of weekenders had more material needs. He began to gather old clothes (a lifelong chore). He made friends with bakers who on

Saturday night might have surplus bread or cake. No matter if it was stale on the Sunday. Hungry boys aren't fussy. In any case, on his Saturday visits to the prisons, he never went empty-handed, using his meagre resources to take fruit, chocolate or tobacco. It broke down barriers and made it easier for him to ask the youngsters to come to see him when they got out.

Gradually the word went round that this rather unusual young priest was genuinely concerned. As he was not working in a parish, he had a certain amount of spare time (in those days!) and this he devoted entirely to his young friends. Some were completely illiterate. He found time to help them. If a boy had a bad employer, he found time to go round his friends, or those of Don Cafasso, in the city, to try to find a better job and a better employer. He was always approachable, always ready to listen. If he made a promise he would see that he kept it. The young rarely forgive a broken promise especially if, as would often be true of these boys, it concerned something of which they were in real need and were relying on. From the start his commitment was complete. He could not help expressing it: "If I had only one piece of bread, I'd share it with you!"

It must be asked what compels even a good man to commit his entire life to such as these boys, boys who, particularly in the early years, were often quite unattractive, unwashed, unkempt, many of them rough in speech and in manners, some crafty with the desperate experience of Fagin's school of rogues, depending entirely on their own resources for survival. The answer must be that Don Bosco, and those like him, saw these boys as Our Lord saw them; "He had compassion on the multitude, for they were lost and bewildered, like sheep without a shepherd". If, as we are taught, God made us to know him, love and serve him in this life and to be happy with him for ever in the next, then these boys, humanly speaking, had little chance, lost, bewildered, exploited in their innocence and ignorance as they were. Without a shepherd they could not survive. God gave Don Bosco a shepherd's mission. He gave him, too, great gifts of nature and of grace, which with the heroicity of a saint, he used to the full. It had to be total commitment.

Someone noted down what he said to the boys one evening after night prayers, some years later.

"I have something important to say to you. I want you to help me in a matter I have very much at heart – your eternal salvation. This is not just the main reason – it is the only reason I am here."

If in later years, he could build houses for them, could feed and clothe them, it was because, having them with him, he could speak to them of God as a loving Father, their loving Father who cared for them. When they got to know God, they could learn to love Him, and loving Him could live as 'good Christian citizens' and die in His grace. So, their eternal salvation, the only object and purpose of his life and work. Let us hope that he won it for them all, for those who responded, those who drifted away, those who fell by the wayside.

Chapter Fourteen

THE WANDERING ORATORY

AS LONG AS Don Bosco could stay with his friends at the Convitto, he could count on it as a centre for his ever growing Oratory. However, his three years came to an end in 1844. Don Cafasso used his influence to get him a post as chaplain to one of the orphanages built and supported by a remarkable lady, the Marchesa de Barolo. Left a widow with an immense fortune, she devoted herself entirely to the provision of homes for the old, the young and those in moral danger. She accepted Don Bosco and allowed him to use the grounds round the latest orphanage while it was being built. But when it was completed she expected him to devote his full time to the general welfare of the girls and leave the noisy boys to someone else. Obviously, quite unthinkable for Don Bosco and they had to part. She, nevertheless, thought a great deal of him and often sent him help through Don Cafasso. Later she offered Don Bosco a substantial sum to take a rest, when she felt his health was suffering. But he declined.

The story for the following year is of every Sunday and Church holiday Don Bosco taking his growing army to some place he had arranged during the week, in and around the city or as far into the country as they could conveniently walk. Turin winters can be harsh and to find a place to pray and play for two hundred lively youngsters in bad weather taxed even Don Bosco's persuasive powers.

The boyhood dream was repeated, perhaps to give him confidence. There was the Lady, the sheep who became boys and now some of the sheep became shepherds. She now showed him of a church, more buildings, and boys in playgrounds.

But the months went by and there was still no sign of any permanent home. However, he gave the Oratory a name, that of the 'Oratory of St. Francis de Sales'. It was important, said Don Cafasso, that the work should have a patron saint and who better than the gentle St. Frances de Sales, a Savoy Saint greatly loved in the Savoy kingdom of Piedmont, a saint too, upon whom Don Bosco tried to model himself. So this naming of the Oratory became the germ, the seed, of the great Salesian Society.

It was in 1845 that he was to meet one who had a fundamental influence on his life and on that of the Society to come. He was one day giving a handful of medals to a small group of boys on the fringes of which was a frail eight year old. The medals ran out by the time the boy got to Don Bosco but the priest smilingly put out his left hand and made as if to cut it in two with his right hand. "We'll go halves," he said. The mystified little lad was Michael Rua, wearing a large mourning ribbon on his arm, as was the custom, for the recent death of his father, and who was then at school with the De La Salle Brothers. Don Bosco did not explain but left the boy puzzling.

Problems mounted up as the year went on. Irate residents complained to the municipality of their Sunday slumbers being violated by these rowdy young ruffians encouraged by that priest, who, said some, ought to be locked up. Friendly parish priests had to withdraw permissions in the face of angry complaints from their parishioners. Farmers who had given permission for some games in unused fields also soon withdrew the permission, saying these hundreds of flying feet killed all the grass. Some parish priests also complained to the church authorities that the Oratory was taking away boys who ought to attend Sunday Mass in their own parishes. Don Bosco pointed out that most of the boys came from outside the city and had no parishes. He would, of course, certainly encourage local boys to go to their own parishes but unless these parishes could provide what the Oratory provided, it was unlikely that many would go. Nor did they.

Matters came to a head on Palm Sunday, 1846. For once Don Bosco sat down during the final games which were being supervised by one or two friends. When the time was up, he would lead a final prayer and then tell the boys where to meet on the following Sunday morning. But today there was nowhere. No-one would have them. This very field was not available for them, nor could he find anywhere in the city or out. It was the end, the end of his dreams ("Ah, those dreams!"). Unless some angel came along to show him what to do, the Oratory was finished. He said afterwards that this was the lowest day of his life.

Then there appeared, not exactly an archangel, but one Pancrazio Soave, stammering and spluttering, from which it appeared that a certain Signor Pinardi had heard the priest was looking for a laboratory ("Not a laboratory, but an Oratory, a little chapel," murmured Don Bosco). They went together to meet the gentleman who was pleased to hear that it was not a laboratory but a chapel because he could sing in the choir himself. There was a long, low shed against the wall of the house. "Far too low," said Don Bosco. "No matter; I'll dig it out half a metre, do repairs, make a floor, have it ready for next week, Easter Sunday" (which he did). "You can have it for 300 lire a year." "Add the ground round it for games and I'll give you 320." "Done; it will be ready." For this sum then, a contract was drawn up between Signor Francesco Pinardi and the Reverend Giovanni Borel, in the district of Valdocco, Turin, for three years. Don Borel signed as guarantor for Don Bosco. That holy man could not get back quickly enough to the boys in the field. "At last, at last, we have a home, a place of our own, no more wanderings!" When all the ecstatic acclamations had died down and Don Bosco had explained exactly where the Pinardi 'shed' was for next Sunday, then and there, and not far from tears, he led them in a thanksgiving prayer to that gracious Lady who was making his dreams at last come true.

Chapter Fifteen

MIRACLE OF THE LITTLE BUILDERS

QUITE EARLY IN his life, Don Bosco felt the need to share his hard won knowledge with all who might need it. Italy was, like the rest of Europe, emerging into literacy and the demand for suitable books was rising. But many were expensive and difficult, with school textbooks sponsored by the State biased on historical and religious grounds. There was need for simple, solid, inexpensive 'books for the masses'. During his time at the Convitto, Don Bosco robbed his sleep of many hours (too many, as he afterwards realised and forbade his Salesians to copy) to provide these books. His first was published in 1845 a CHURCH HISTORY FOR SCHOOLS: it became the accepted textbook throughout the country; it was simple, clear, interesting, perhaps not brilliant but factual depending on its author's industry and prodigious memory. Other 'best sellers' followed. In 1847, a BIBLE HISTORY, in 1849, a HISTORY OF ITALY correcting many distortions regarding the Church. Oddly enough, in 1855, there was the METRIC SYSTEM. One would have thought it was not a priest's job to instruct the people as a whole but the guides provided by the Government were not, it seems, clear. It was brief, clearly illustrated with examples and was country-wide popular. In spite of the enormous demands on his time, night after night Don Bosco scratched away by the light of candle or small oil lamp, producing a whole shelf of books. No wonder, in view of his constant battle against time, the handwriting was generally atrocious; later, younger eyes would decipher it with love, transcribing it for the press.

To go back to the Pinardi 'shed'. As the first sign of stability, it was the first small reply to a host of critics and doubting friends. Possibly a little indiscreetly, for some years Don Bosco had been encouraging his young followers with his dreams of a glorious future. "Oh, one day there would be fine schools, workshops, splendid churches, and not only in Turin!" Many of his fellow priests affected to be seriously disturbed by these 'castles in the air' fancies. Surely the poor man must be suffering from delusions! A solemn, private gathering of grave ecclesiastics decided he needed what we call psychiatric treatment, and planned to get him into a mental hospital for the purpose.

Accordingly two venerable Fathers called on their dear young friend Don Bosco to invite him for a ride in the country. Their coach was at the door. But Don Bosco had been forewarned. "A ride in the country? By all means, how kind of you! I must get my hat." He accompanied them to the coach, "Seniores priores! After you, Fathers!" As soon as the elderly clerics had climbed in, he slammed the door shut, calling out to the coachman, "Off you go, my friend, as fast as you can, to the mental hospital!" And off they galloped, in fine style, with the painful results at the hospital that can well be imagined. The story swept gleefully round the diocese, not without some embroidering.

Many still thought the young priest was quite mad in his illusions, but perhaps it would be well to treat him with care. However, there could seem to be some foundation for their doubts when rumours spread that he was ill.

The Marchesa de Barolo, older and more experienced, had not been deceived. Don Bosco was certainly ill; his coughing was incessant and he began to spit blood. On the first Sunday of July, 1846, three months after taking over the Pinardi property, after a killing day in the scorching sun, he collapsed. The Marchesa at once sent doctors and nurses. He was exhausted, worn out, and soon there was cause for alarm. He grew worse and the doctors advised that he be given the last Sacraments. The word went through the streets, into the factories and the building sites. Don Bosco was dying.

Salesian biographers speak of what followed as the 'miracle of the little builders, the apprentices'. They came in droves, begging, in vain, to be admitted to the sick room. They came in their rough clothes, after twelve hours' work, without eating, weeping teenagers kneeling on the steps, filling the little Pinardi chapel, begging, beseeching God for the life of their father. Many made, in their generous grief, rash promises; they would pray all night, they would live on bread and water for a week, they would say the rosary every day for a year, anything, to win Don Bosco's life from Heaven. After eight or nine days, the crisis came: and passed. The 'miracle had happened'.

On the last Sunday of that anxious July, Don Bosco, leaning on his stick, was able to walk slowly down to the Oratory. The boys met him and swept him up to carry him into the little chapel. There they offered their prayers of thanksgiving, to God and to Our Lady. He managed to say a few words, few but perhaps the most significant of his life. "My dear boys, I owe my life to you, to your prayers. But be certain of this; from now on I promise to spend every moment of that life for you!" Says Father Teresio Bosco, this was a solemn vow of consecration, in words only equalled by those uttered on his deathbed forty-two years later. "Tell my boys, that I shall be waiting for them all in heaven!"

The doctors prescribed a long convalescence. But before he left for home, that of his mother and brother Joseph at the Becchi, he called together those boys who had made over-generous promises in their prayers for his recovery. To set their consciences at rest, he used his priestly powers to change all their austerities into simple little offerings, soon given. Then he told them all. "Now I am going home for a while. But don't worry! By the fall of the leaves, I shall be back again with you!"

Chapter Sixteen

BACK WITH THE FALL OF THE LEAVES

BACK FIRST, TO the fields, the vines of the Becchi, with the fresh fruit and vegetables, with Mamma Margaret's homemade bread, and brother Joseph's rich red Barbera to make every meal a feast, all this and the fresh air, soon brought life into Don Bosco's lungs and limbs. Anthony's wife and five children welcomed him with as much love and enthusiasm as did Joseph's wife and four, with Grandma Margaret presiding over all. For the children there never was such an uncle as their Uncle John, with all his stories and a hundred tricks to pass the evenings, now beginning to close in. Boys and girls would vie with one another to accompany him on well-loved walks, to call in on farms where he would be welcomed with delight and the regaling of old tales and memories of his boyhood escapades.

However, once he was returning alone as evening fell, when from the shade of a wayside thicket, a menacing voice stopped him. "Stand still and let's see your money if you want to go on living!" Don Bosco was as alarmed as any of us would be on being confronted by a muffled up figure holding a long knife. But as he was stammering out that he had no money, he recognised the voice.

"Why, you are Cortese, and you are threatening to take my life?"

"Oh, Don Bosco, forgive me! I never thought I would meet you out here! You were so good to me in the prison. But everything has gone wrong: I lost my job, and, there was nothing for it but this. I don't know what I can do!" and the youngster's plaints dissolved into tears. Don Bosco took him home, introducing him as one of his young Turin friends. He sent him off in the morning with a letter for Don Cafasso about the possibility of getting a job.

A Mother in the House

Letters from Don Cafasso and Don Borel told him they had taken three rooms in the Pinardi house ready for his return. There was however, a difficulty. The Valdocco district had a bad reputation in the city and for a young priest to live there alone could give rise to unwelcome comment.

Once again, Don Bosco thought of his mother. She was probably never better off in her life than she was then, living in Joseph's house, a good friend and helpful companion to his wife, without any real responsibility or worry. To ask her to leave all this now, at fifty-eight, and take over at Valdocco, was hard indeed. But she knew what her Don Giovanni would be up against. Obviously, the safest solution would be for his mother to keep house for him. So after a struggle, she agreed, packed up her bits and pieces including her wedding dress, her one treasure and, as the last leaves were falling on a November morning, set off, mother and son, to walk the fifteen odd miles to Turin, no mean jaunt. Salesian legend tells us that when they were wearily approaching the suburbs, they met a Don Vola, an old friend, who was both delighted and shocked to see them.

"Why, you've had to walk from the Becchi! Now you have no salary? And what are you going to live on when you get to Valdocco?" Don Bosco smiled. "I don't know, but Providence will look after us. We'll get by somehow!" Don Vola shook his head.

"You're just as crazy as ever you were, John! Well, I'm sorry I just haven't got any money on me, but, well, perhaps this will bring you in a bit to get started," and he handed them, insisting they take it, his valuable gold watch and chain, probably belonging to his father, and much treasured. For which quite heroic act of generosity, we trust the recording angel made mention in letters of gold.

When they opened the door at the Pinardi house and looked into the bare rooms, unfurnished except for a table, two chairs and the two beds in the bedrooms, Don Bosco laughed.

"Well, Mother, you said that if I ever became a rich priest, you would not darken my door. I don't think you could get anything much poorer than this, now could you?" She smiled back, content just to be with him, no matter what the future might hold. Later, a boy passing the house, saw a light, and heard two voices, singing an evening hymn. "He's back!" he whispered, and sped off into the city streets, bringing the good news.

Chapter Seventeen

NEW POPE, FIRST ORPHANS AND POLITICAL EXPLOSIONS

IN THAT SAME year of 1846, a most profound influence in the affairs of Don Bosco entered history. Cardinal Mastai-Ferretti, known as 'a simple priest who loved humanity,' was elected Pope, taking the title of Pius IX. In those days the Pope was the prince ruler of the Papal States, covering the centre of Italy; he had a parliament, a prime minister, an army. His was one of the eight independent States that made up what we know as Italy today.

Pope Pius IX had much of the 'good Pope John' approach to his exalted position. He began by freeing all political prisoners. He would often slip out to the mean streets of Rome to see how his people lived, he would visit the hospitals, see how they were run, as well as bless the sick.

For Don Bosco he proved a rock of support; Piedmont priest and Roman Pope built up a remarkable relationship. Today, if you walk down the right aisle in St. Peter's, Rome, as far as the seated statue of St. Peter (kiss his foot!) and then look straight up, you will see that the large plaque is of Pius IX and further up still is the huge statue of St. John Bosco and Dominic Savio. Even today they are very close!

First Orphans

Don Bosco never had any money, of course, chiefly because he spent it before he got it. Debts were a way of life with him and did not for a moment stop him expanding. Over the winter of 1846/7, he took over the whole Pinardi house and started evening classes. Soon every room in the house, every corner including the stairs and the kitchen, was packed with boys with their noses in books. Spare time helpers shared the work of teaching and correction.

We have said that Valdocco was a rough area and many rowdy gangs made the nights hideous; sometimes they would throw stones at the house, try to disrupt the chapel services. More than once Don Bosco had to sally forth to quell the disturbances; in the dark he was smashed in the face and had to fight himself free of attackers. True, that dream had said "Not by blows will you tame these rough boys . . . ." But sometimes even dreams have their exceptions.

He was well aware that these boys could keep his mother awake half the night because they had no homes to go to. He tried to help. There was a little passageway adjacent to the house where he and his mother made up a dozen straw beds and blankets and offered them to one group. They sent them to rest with hot soup; but when Don Bosco went to see how they had fared he found they had all decamped, taking bowls and blankets with them. A second attempt also failed.

The First Orphan Boarder

Came a night when it was raining in torrents. There was a timid knock at the door. A small figure stood there, drenched to the skin, shivering and weeping.

"Who are you, son?" Margaret asked.

"I'm an orphan. I had three lire when I came to the city but it's all gone and I've nowhere to go."

"Well, come in out of the rain and we'll see what we can do."

Don Bosco found some clothes for him to wear while he was getting through soup and bread and his own clothes were drying. He was plainly apprehensive.

"I've nowhere to go. Please don't send me away."

"We might find somewhere for you to stay," said Margaret, "but the last boys we gave a bed to ran off with all the blankets. What about you?"

"Oh, not me! I may be poor but I've never been a thief."

He was the first 'boarder'. Soon another boy was at the door.

"My mother died yesterday and the landlord threw me out; he said he was going to keep our things because Mum hadn't paid any rent."

Another boy, a Carlo Gastini, who had been one of Don Bosco's Oratory boys for some years, came with the same story.

"My mother died yesterday, my brother is in the army far away, and I don't know what to do." Carlo stayed with Don Bosco all his life, was the great organiser of concerts and comedies and always said he'd live to seventy because Don Bosco had told him he would. He died in 1902, aged seventy and one day.

A fourth was the immortal Giuseppe Buzzetti, who just wanted to be with Don Bosco. By the end of the winter there were eight.

The Archbishop's Mitre

On June 21st, feast of St. Aloysius, patron of youth, Archbishop Fransoni came to the Oratory to say Mass and administer confirmation to those who lacked it. When he climbed into the simple pulpit, the low Pinardi roof almost knocked his mitre off. He took it calmly. "One has to show respect to Don Bosco's boys and preach with head uncovered!"

The giggling boys warmed to him. So did Don Bosco when the Archbishop signed the necessary documents for the confirmation, naming the place as 'the parish of abandoned children'. That was valuable support for Don Bosco in a matter in which certain of his colleagues disagreed with him.

Europe Explodes

Not that the Archbishop himself was without troubles. The Spring of 1848 found all Piedmont, indeed all Italy, in ferment. Political demonstrations were drawing thousands, demanding the end of the independent states, including the Papal States. In Turin, eighty seminarians demanded the right to take part. The Archbishop refused permission, seeing the hand of international anti-clerical Liberalism behind the organisation. The eighty seminarians went anyway, and shouted with the rest. Whereupon the Archbishop closed the seminary. But by the end of that year of 1848, all Europe was in flames.

Karl Marx had issued his 'Communist Manifesto' that year; red revolution spread like a forest fire. Monarchs were tumbled off their thrones, barricades went up in city streets. It was a revolt chiefly of the working classes, victims of the industrial revolution; the peasants from country areas took little part and were generally not in favour.

There was a 'copycat' pattern about the uprisings. In February all Paris went up in savage battles; Vienna erupted on March 13th, Berlin and Budapest on the 15th, Venice on the 17th and Milan on the 18th. At the start, there were sweeping victories for the insurgents, but terrible losses when the trained army counterattacked not hesitating to use their cannon on the workers, workers being men, women and children, marking with their blood their first concerted protest at the inhuman conditions of their work, against employers demanding twelve, fourteen and more hours a day for starvation wages, six days a week. Thousands were said to have died, before some sort of order was restored.

Protests in Italy, were, of course, concerned equally with the industrial ills and with the demand for a new Constitution and resistance to Austrian threats of war. Pope Pius IX supported the Piedmontese Charles Albert against Austrian claims and offered 17,000 papal troops in support. He also prayed for 'all Italy'. "Bless, great God, all Italy and preserve in her the priceless gift of the faith!" The popular press took this up, this blessing for 'all Italy' while ignoring the plea for the preservation of the faith. The Pope was everywhere hailed as a 'liberal Pope'. But when the war ended in defeat for Charles Albert, the Pope was found not to be liberal enough and soon the mobs were baying for his blood.

Chapter Eighteen

MADNESS IN THE AIR BUT GOD'S IN HIS HEAVEN

IN SPITE OF Don Bosco's desperate efforts to keep clear of politics, ("My politics are those of the Our Father,") politics would not keep clear of him; because he would not join in the popular demonstrations, his Pinardi home was attacked by stone-throwing mobs, a terrifying experience he had to suffer more than once. Liberal papers attacked him, as they did the Church in general and the Archbishop in particular, who was eventually forced to flee to Switzerland. The Jesuits and the Sisters, 'the Dames of the Sacred Heart,' were also attacked, pillaged by mobs and forced to abandon their homes. The Convitto, quiet oasis of study and work for the prisons and the poor, was ringed by mobs, shouting, "Death to Don Guala!" though it was beyond the mind of man to understand how *he* could have merited such a fate. Even the Marchesa, benefactress indeed to the whole city of Turin with her hospitals, homes for the old, orphanages for the young, even she had her windows smashed and her life threatened.

There was madness in the air throughout that year of 1848 and after. Even some younger clergy were led away by the 'patriotic frenzy'. When two of Don Bosco's temporary helpers took it upon themselves to preach 'patriotic' sermons to his Oratory boys, he could not help but remonstrate with them. Whereupon they turned back to the boys and led 400 of them away in triumph through the streets, leaving a saddened Don Bosco and his one faithful friend, Don Borel, alone with the remaining 100.

Later many of the younger ones returned to the Oratory. So full were they of ideas of the 'war of independence against Austria' that he thought he would turn it into a game by getting an ex-army friend to drill them with mock guns. It was not one of his better ideas, though well meant. The old sergeant decided they would have a mock battle and divided the 'army' into friend and foe. When he gave the order to attack, chaos ensued; the battle swayed to and fro, eventually over Mamma Margaret's precious kitchen garden. Not only was it trampled to destruction but cabbages, tomatoes, onions were pulled up and used as ammunition. When all was over, the poor woman could only look upon the devastation in tears, tears not far from Don Bosco's eyes as he looked with her. It was the more tragic because food was becoming scarce and prices rising everywhere.

A touch of real war came shortly after. When Don Bosco was talking to the boys in the chapel, someone crept up to the window and fired at him from short range. The ball, a rough piece of iron fired from a musket, passed between his side and his arm, ripping his cassock. The boys screamed in fear, the priest, trying to calm them, remarking, "This is my only cassock, a pity to tear it! But Our Lady is looking after us, never fear!" Someone fired a pistol at the little Don Borel but fortunately missed him, too.

As that dark year moved into a grey November, news came from Rome that a frenzied mob had murdered the Pope's moderate Prime Minister, Pellegrino Rossi. A fortnight later, Pius IX, dressed as a simple priest, early one morning walked out of the Vatican, on his way to 'exile' to a villa in Gaeta, not far from Naples. It did indeed seem to the embattled Church and its frightened people that the powers of evil were beginning to triumph.

All was certainly not right in the world; but there was a God in Heaven and two reminders came to Don Bosco, two rays of hope.

One of his boys, Ascanio Savio, asked to receive the clerical habit. Since the seminary was now closed, the Archbishop allowed him to stay on with Don Bosco, to study and give what spare time help he could. This was the first of the sheep to become a shepherd. He became eventually a diocesan priest but remained a lifelong friend of Don Bosco.

The second sign of God's approval was entirely different. Don Bosco had long wanted to get away from the Jansenistic idea that, so unworthy are we, once a year was sufficient to receive Holy Communion. He encouraged his boys to communicate often; we need food for our souls as well as our bodies. On an important feast day of the Church he had urged the boys to please God by making a good Holy Communion and when he turned to the tabernacle to bring out the ciborium, large numbers of the boys came forward to the altar rails. Judge of his dismay when he found the ciborium with but a pitiful few hosts remaining. That good young man, Giuseppe Buzzetti, (of course, what didn't he do!) had forgotten to put out a fresh ciborium and now looked with dismay as he saw Don Bosco's face. The distribution began with what hosts there were, Giuseppe holding the communion plate and waiting for the end in great distress. But as the first row ended and then another, it was obvious that something was happening. Don Bosco appears to have given out what would have been a full ciborium and when he finished there were still the few original hosts left. Years afterwards, in 1864, Giuseppe told the story once again to a group of Salesians.

Don Bosco, asked point-blank, admitted the miracle. "Yes," he said, "there were only a few Hosts in the ciborium unfortunately, but I was able to distribute Holy Communion to all who came and there were many. I was moved to see what was happening but not disturbed. I reflected that, after all, the miracle of the consecration is far greater than a simple multiplication. But it was, just then, a comforting sign of God's continuing care for us."

Actually that year there was another moving example of what some called a 'little miracle for the simple poor'. It is attested by two who witnessed it: once more Buzzetti and a boy called Tomatis. It was the custom in those parts to go to the cemetery on All Souls Day, to pray for the souls of the dead. On that Sunday, November 4th, Don Bosco promised a good handful of hot chestnuts for all who came and quite a small army went with him. To keep his promise he had bought three sacks of sweet chestnuts and asked his mother to cook them. But apparently, she did not understand that there would be so many with him and cooked only one large pot. Buzzetti, in charge at home, found out too late.

When Don Bosco arrived with the hordes of cold and expectant boys, he took what he thought to be the first pot of cooked nuts and began to ladle them out with fine abandon. Buzzetti tried to stop him.

"Oh, Don Bosco, not so fast! There'll not be enough to go round!"

"What! Not enough? But I bought three sackfuls!"

"Yes, but only that one pot was cooked!"

"Oh, well, we'll just have to go on as far as they will go," and on he went with the big ladle.

The anxious boys watched him with some alarm when no second or third pot arrived. They grew silent as they continued to file past him, their two hands held out for the warm nuts. The ladle came out each time full, until the last boy was served. A murmur began to go round the yard. "Did you see? Don Bosco must be a saint!" Again it could not be gainsaid and, every year after, hot chestnuts were distributed on All Souls Day in memory of the event. We can see it as gentle proof of Our Father in Heaven's smiling concern for the least and simplest of his children.

"Fear not, little flock! Not a sparrow falls but that your Father in Heaven marks it;.but you are worth more than many sparrows!"

Chapter Nineteen

THE POOR MAN MUST BE QUITE CRAZY!

THE YEAR 1849 began badly for Don Bosco. His stepbrother, Anthony, aged only forty-one died, leaving seven children. For years they had been good friends and Anthony was a frequent visitor to the Oratory.

In the city there was a Catholic reaction when 1,000 clergy and 10,000 lay-people sent a petition to the Senate requesting the return of the Archbishop. Mgr. Fransoni soon reappeared but when the Senate passed a law restricting the rights of the Church and seeking to replenish its coffers at the expense of the Church, he vigorously protested. He was arrested, fined, imprisoned, and finally banished again.

Nothing daunted, Don Bosco, who was now boarding and feeding thirty homeless boys, in addition to his Oratory, made a petition to the Senate for a subsidy for his work. It brought in 300 lire from them and 2,000 from the Minister of the Interior, Urban Rattazzi, whom we shall meet again.

It was about this time that the Oratory boys, after hearing Don Bosco speak of the Pope in exile, collected the sum of thirty-three lire, which was sent to Gaeta, with a loyal letter. Pius IX never forgot this simple act, the 'mite' from the youngest and poorest; he sent a parcel of 720 rosaries for them, which took more than a year to arrive!

Meanwhile Don Bosco began to think again of that dream, 'sheep becoming shepherds'. If his work was going to expand he must get help from his own resources. He spoke to four of the more promising boys and asked them if they would like to study Italian (most of them spoke only the Piedmontese dialect) and Latin, with the possibility one day of the priesthood. They agreed and worked for eighteen months; but only one, Buzzetti, of course, stayed with Don Bosco and he became years later, a laybrother. But there were others and with another four there was more success. Don Bosco had kept his eyes on that Michael Rua whom he had mystified with his "We'll go halves". Now grown tall but still somewhat frail, he was thinking of starting work. Don Bosco spoke to the mother about Latin for Michael; she agreed but while the boy stayed with Don Bosco, she brought him home to feed him, to try to build him up a little, for the next two years. In the meantime, Michael helped with the younger boys for games and classes. Another one of this second four picked out by Don Bosco was the twelve year old Francesia, who became a renowned Salesian Latinist and lived until 1930, when the present writer had already been a year in the Salesian fold! Such is continuity!

Sheep becoming shepherds was part of the preparation for the future; now there must be material progress. The Pinardi house was rented, a somewhat precarious base. Catching Francesco Pinardi one day, Don Bosco said, "I'd like to buy the house off you". "All right," said Pinardi, "65,000." Don Bosco laughed, "I have had it valued and they give me the figure of between 26,000 and 28,000 lire; I'll offer you 30,000 for immediate sale". "In cash and all at once?" "Yes." "And within a fortnight?" "Done." They shook hands. Don Bosco's head began to swim. He hadn't a bean and here he was pledging himself to find 30,000 lire in two weeks! No wonder people said he was crazy! But he had complete trust; and how it was rewarded! To have a rough idea of values, it must be said that the Italian lira was worth much less than the U.S. dollar at the time; but as a rough and ready comparison, if we take a lira to a dollar today, we shall not be far out. Thus 30,000 dollars of today's money would be a fair estimate for the rundown old farmhouse.

That very evening Don Cafasso came in saying that a pious lady, the Countess Riccardi, had given him 10,000 lire to be used 'for the glory of God'. He could think of no better use for it than Don Bosco's need. They looked further. The next day came a Rosminian Father bringing a loan of 20,000 lire from Don Rosmini himself; the interest was to be four percent; Don Bosco later remarked that at no time did the great priest seek either interest or capital. A Count Cotta offered a further 3,000 to cover essential expenses. Providence had stepped in swiftly indeed!

But as for Don Bosco, there was no holding the man! That same month, he remarked casually to his mother, "You know, I'd like to build a fine church in honour of St. Francis of Sales". Margaret dropped the needle and thread on her lap. "A church? And you can't feed the boys without getting into debt! Where's the money going to come from, may I ask?"

"Mother, if you had the money, would you give it to me? Of course you would; well, God is even more generous than you and I am sure He will give it to us."

Margaret sighed; "What can you do with a son like that! Quite crazy!"

It was true that the Pinardi chapel was no longer serviceable; it was cold, damp, in poor state and liable to flooding in bad weather; and it was by now far too small for the hundreds of boys. As usual, Don Bosco lost no time. He had immediate plans drawn up. To the contractor he said he wanted the work to go ahead without delay although he had as yet no money. "If you have no money, we'll have to go slow." "No, I want it built in the year; we need it as soon as possible." "That may be, but you'll have to find the money to keep us going."

"When the foundations had been dug," Don Bosco records, "we had the blessing of the foundation stone on July 20th, 1851. Our great benefactor, Count Cotta, laid it, the complimentary address was read by the young Michael Rua, aged fourteen, and the famous preacher, Padre Barrera, gave the address, in the course of which he said, 'This stone is the grain of mustard seed. It will grow into a great tree, in which many boys will find shelter'."

Don Bosco and his friends knocked at doors far and wide. He collected 35,000 lire, still 30,000 short. He decided to run a gigantic public lottery. He went on knocking on doors for gifts, sparing neither the Queen Mother nor the Court itself. With eventually 3,300 prizes it must have been a 'gigantic' effort! Don Bosco always thought big! The lottery made 26,000 lire: the rest eventually came in. The church was consecrated on June 20th, 1852 inside a year; it is the 'Salesian Porziuncula' and for 16 years in its walls beat the heart of Don Bosco's work. It is still there, though overshadowed, from 1868, by the great bulk of the Basilica of Maria Ausiliatrice; but that must wait its own story.

For the next four years until her death, Margaret Bosco knelt daily at her 'crazy' son's Mass, growing old and weary but ever marvelling at God's mysterious and wonderful ways.

Chapter Twenty
GOD SENT A DOG!

IN 1848 THE Piedmont Senate voted to give religious freedom to all religions, sects and denominations; there had previously been some restrictions, with the Catholic religion the state religion. Far from accepting the lifting of the restrictions with relief and satisfaction, certain extreme sects began a campaign of attacks on Catholic teaching. Three newspapers appeared, possibly financed from outside the country, and achieved a wide circulation, vilifying the Catholic clergy, falsifying history, calumniating individuals. The Bishops and clergy called for replies to these attacks, to protect the laity from these false prophets. Don Bosco was one of the first to take up the challenge. With a group of collaborators, he began CATHOLIC READINGS of which he wrote and published the first six issues himself. He pulled no punches, answering all the attacks and showing them to be false; there was no compromise, it was hard wall-to-wall attack and counterattack: The READINGS were welcomed everywhere and sales increased with every issue.

The success of this Catholic reply did not, of course, go unnoticed as did not the person of its vigorous leader. His name came in for sarcastic comment and veiled threats. In his brief Memoirs, Don Bosco himself recalled how one day two respectable gentlemen asked to see him and began to talk about the READINGS. They praised his contributions and his evident knowledge of history and scripture. They knew of his books for the schools. Would it not be better to produce more such helpful books, and leave the tiresome squabbles in the READINGS to others? True, there might be some financial difficulty here; they knew he had many commitments in his work for destitute youth; well, there were a couple of thousand lire notes on the table which might help . . . Don Bosco concluded the interview, asking Buzzetti to accompany these two gentlemen to the gate. They went quietly but not without suggesting he would regret his refusal to keep quiet.

So, having survived political attacks, he was now to be the target for sectarian attempts on his life. He was advised not to walk out alone but to take some of the older boys with him. Twice he was called out to bogus sick calls. At one house he was offered wine and chestnuts and when he declined, the 'sick' person's family tried to force him to drink and that from a 'special' bottle. When he called in his boys and suggested they take the wine and the chestnuts, the farce ended, it was all 'a joke'. In another house at the bedside of a supposedly dying person, that worthy began a violent row with bystanders and in the resultant melee, the priest had to defend himself with a chair until the boys burst in to rescue him.

However, one night he was returning home alone when to his alarm an enormous dog appeared at his side, walking with him, as if he were its owner. "We soon established an amicable relationship and he escorted me home." Don Bosco called him Grigio, the grey one. Once when he was out, again alone, he noticed two men keeping pace with him, quickening if he did, slowing as he did. He made as if to turn back but they jumped on him, trying to envelop him in a heavy cloak, possibly to drag him off. But then there was a tremendous howl and a great body dashed against them, growling fiercely, 'like a mad wolf'. The men screamed in terror and Don Bosco had to call Grigio off to save them from serious injury before they fled.

Michael Rua, who saw the dog twice, recalls how one evening, when Don Bosco was preparing to go out alone in spite of his mother's entreaties, he found Grigio at the door barring his way. No matter how he tried he could not get past, Grigio with low growls pushing against him. Margaret cried out, "If you won't listen to me, for goodness' sake listen to the dog!" Later that night a neighbour came in to say that a man had been seen nearby, carrying a pistol. There is no doubt that Grigio's very appearance with Don Bosco prevented many attacks.

Another time Grigio came in through the playground gate, somewhat to the alarm of some of the boys. Buzzetti cried out, "Leave him alone, he's Don Bosco's dog!" The dog went on and finally into the refectory where Don Bosco was having supper with a few students. Grigio went up to him, put his great head on his knees, as if to say 'Good night' before leaving; it was noticed that, unlike most dogs, he refused all food. It looked as if he wanted to assure himself that Don Bosco was safe at home; he had missed him because the priest had been given a lift home in a friend's carriage.

One of the boys who saw him described Grigio as a huge wolfhound, with erect ears, long pointed nose, grey pelt and a metre high. (A metre = three feet three inches; some dog!) Salesian legend speaks of other appearances of Grigio over some years. When a Baroness Fassati asked Don Bosco point-blank where he came from, the priest smiled, "Well, to say he was some sort of angel is silly; but certainly, he was no ordinary dog!"

Chapter Twenty-One

WORKSHOPS AND APPRENTICE CONTRACTS

THE STAMMERING, LITTLE man Pancrazio Soave wasn't really very far out when he thought the priest was looking for a place for a 'laboratorio'; the 'oratorio' came first and then the laboratorio, which is what the Italians call a workshop. As soon as the church was paid off, the unceasing flow of homeless boys knocking at the Pinardi door urged Don Bosco to add a sizeable extension to the house. When it was nearly finished, one night the whole thing collapsed. Popular estimation was that the devil was trying to prevent the good being done; be that as it may, the immediate cause was shoddy work, the cheapest materials, the poor cement; poor Don Bosco had to learn at the cost of 10,000 hard won lire that the lowest estimate is not always the best investment. But he needed the rooms, so, another estimate and a better eye on the builders.

He had to decide what he was going to do with these boys. Basic education he gave them all; those who gave any hope of a vocation, such as Michael Rua, he sent off to a school run by a Don Bonzanino; schools existed but attendance was not compulsory. He had to do something else for those who could not and did not want to study. Now his own experiences as a teenager trying to pick up what expertise he might, came to the fore. One day he bought two rough work benches, four chairs, a few lasts and showed four boys how to hammer a leather sole as it should be hammered. Soon they were all four hammering away and the first workshop, the shoemakers, was on its way. Then the tailors. He had spent some time with the good Signor Roberto in Castelnuovo with so much profit that a partnership was even discussed. So, for another four boys and four more chairs from the kitchen, they began the preliminaries. Patching, mending first, with Margaret's practical expertise with needle and cotton forming the basis. Then Don Bosco remembered his cutting out and by 1853, this workshop was going well, and was popular.

Early in 1854, he one day received the sheets of his latest book, THE GUARDIAN ANGEL. Some boys helped him carry the heavy package into the kitchen. "Right," he said, pointing to one startled youngster, "You are the bookbinder!" "What, me? I don't even know what a bookbinder is!" "Quite simple! Let's take the first big sheet. Fold it into two; and fold it again, carefully; and again, and still again; and once more. It looks like a little book, now, doesn't it? Now each sheet, we'll say, is a chapter of the book; look for the page number and put all the same sheets together, in order. Now you try the folding; be careful to make it an exact fold!" When all was more or less satisfactory, Margaret brought a big darning needle and good thread and showed them how to stitch the sections together. "Right; now let's get some flour and water from the kitchen and make a good paste to fix the cover," the cover being of paper with the printed title. To trim the edges, Don Bosco sharpened the heavy knife Margaret used for topping and tailing the carrots, etc. and made a fair job. A little primitive, but it served to start. That was workshop number three. When things were well on the way. Don Bosco, of course, engaged experienced craftsmen to supervise the work in all the trades.

By 1856, Don Bosco had built a large shed for workshop number four, the carpenters and joiners. You need a fair amount of room for woodwork and he made this shop as well equipped as he could with simple machinery. This, too, soon flourished.

The most important of his workshops in his 'School of Arts and Trades' was the printing department. In those suspicious days, no-one was allowed to open a printer's shop without a license and it took Don Bosco a long time and much talking before he got his; the date was December 31st, 1861. Such a printing press could be a powerhouse of support for religion, for faith and morals, for defence of justice and peace throughout the land. By the middle of the year 1862, this 'Press of the Oratory of St. Francis de Sales' was printing and publishing the CATHOLIC READINGS and continued to do so for years. The modest start in Valdocco was the precursor of a chain of Salesian printers the world over who can now compete with the most modern. Workshop number six also started in that year of 1862, with the mechanics department; in these days of course, they talk of computers, television, silicon chips! But no doubt, 2,000 years ago, St. Joseph had to mend and make sandals, make furniture, use iron and hardwood in the simple ploughs; and Our Lady spent her spare hours at the spinning wheel, weaving the cloth and sewing together her husband's clothes and those of Her Son Jesus. Don Bosco was always conscious of the sanctity of good work and founded the Sodality of St. Joseph for all his working boys. They were free to join or not, but many did. But when the boys had learnt the rudiments at Valdocco, it was time for some of them to go out and get a job, first as apprentices.

In the Salesian archives are preserved two rare documents, relating to contracts drawn up between the employer, the apprentice and witnessed by Don Bosco, dated 1851 and 1852. He was not the inventor of apprentice contracts but in practice few people bothered about them, the boys' parents being often illiterate and ignorant of the boys' rights; nor did the Liberal state help. ("There must be freedom even in these matters.") But the two documents show Don Bosco's practical concern for his boys; after all, most of them were orphans and he was 'in loco parentis'. He was responsible. We see how a Turin jeweller undertook to take this sixteen year old orphan under his care for three years, to teach him the art without making him do extraneous work, would leave him free on Sundays and holy days of obligation, and would give him fifteen days paid holiday every year. If he had to take the boy to task for some misdemeanor, he must admonish him in words only, and not by beating him; he must treat him, 'da padre e non da padrone,' that is, 'as a father' and not as a master, a hard employer. Furthermore, his pay must increase each year as the boy became more proficient. One rate given was two lire a week for the first year, four for the second and eight for the third year, which would be comparable to a normal wage. No Trade Union could do better for apprentices! Not only that but both Don Bosco and the Salesian Brothers would keep an eye on the boys and see that the terms of the contracts were honoured.

Chapter Twenty-Two
SCHOOLBOYS IN ARMY COATS

BUT NOW LET us meet perhaps the most sparkling star in the whole Salesian firmament! Don Bosco was giving the sermon on the Feast of All Saints, 1851 in his hometown Castelnuovo. A small boy sat in the front row with his mother; all through the talk, he fixed his eyes on the priest, staring at him while the Mass went on. The priest met him. "Is there anything you want to say to me, young man?" "Yes; I want to go to Turin with you, go to school and become a priest." "Well, that's clear enough; we'll have to ask your Mum." Mum was a young widow whom Don Bosco had known as a girl. (How many widows do we meet in this Don Bosco story!)

"Teresa," asked Don Bosco, "How much will you sell me your son for?" She laughed, "In these parts we sell our calves and lambs; our sons we give away". "Well, pack up a few clean clothes in a bundle he can carry and we'll get off first thing in the morning." The dawn was hardly in the sky before Giovani Cagliero was up, had his breakfast, kissed his mother and with his bundle on his back, was knocking at Don Bosco's door. "Well, when do we start?" They set off for the long walk to Turin, about fifteen miles. At least Don Bosco did the fifteen miles; the will-of-the-wisp Giovanni, chasing a butterfly up the road and a dragonfly across a field and back, did twice the distance. As a priest, he told the story himself.

"Don Bosco asked me a thousand questions and I gave him a thousand answers, all about myself. Since then I've never had a secret from him. He laughed at all my pranks and said I'd have to quieten down in the city. At last we got to Valdocco, very tired. We went in. Don Bosco said to his mother. 'Let me present to you a young man from Castelnuovo!' His mother sighed. 'All you do is bring me more and more boys and there's just nowhere to put them!' 'Well, this one is so small that we can put him in a canary cage and hoist him up and down from the rafters!' which made them both laugh. There wasn't any room that I could see and I spent the first night lying at the feet of another boy. In the morning I saw the poverty of the place. We ate in a shed; there were some tin bowls and tin spoons; such things as knives and forks and tablecloths did not appear for years. Don Bosco was everywhere;

he served us at table, dishing out the food, helping to clear up after, mending our boots, patching our clothes; it was a real home, with a father who loved us and cared only for our spiritual and bodily welfare."

Michael Rua came to live in about that time and Don Bosco gave him the job of being in charge of the little group going to Don Bonzanino's school. But he could never put a bridle on Cagliero. As soon as they got outside the gate, he skipped away, racing through the market, laughing at the jugglers and the buskers; but when the group got to the school there he was, red in the face, before them. Rua disapproved. "Why can't you come with us?"

"If I want to go another way, and look at a few things, what's the difference?"

"You should do as you are told."

"I do. I am told to go to school. Here I am. I am told not to be late, I am always here before you. So what?"

Rua, quiet, serious, steady, Cagliero, extrovert, exuberant, sparkling, two pillars of the Salesian Society. Rua the first Salesian, first successor of Don Bosco, Cagliero shortly after him, the first missionary, the first Salesian Bishop, the first Salesian Cardinal. Both of them would have died for Don Bosco.

Schoolboys in Army Jackets

Winters can be bitter in Italy and Don Bosco wrote to the Ministry for War for discarded army clothes for the boys. The earliest photograph, in 1861, shows some of them wearing army jackets and caps. The overcoats were somewhat worse for wear and when the well-to-do sons of Turin Society in Don Bonzanino's saw the scruffy group from Valdocco, they turned their noses up. Fees were high for those who could pay; for Don Bosco, there was no charge. "We're a school for young gentlemen and young tramps," sang the boys. Don Bonzanino would have none of it. "What matters here is what you have in your heads, not what you have on your backs!" Indeed, because the Valdocco boys had no 'social distractions,' they worked hard and their results were uniformly brilliant, to Don Bonzanino's great satisfaction. And Don Bosco's.

Fifty years Guarantee of Life

One day Michael Rua and Giovanni (John) Francesia were having a discussion, though there was little coming from Rua. Francesia lost patience; they were two kindred souls and it was not like Rua to be silent.

"What's the matter with you?" "My brother John has died and I'm the last one. It'll be my turn next." Don Bosco was standing by. He had just written a pamphlet on the Turin miracle of the Blessed Sacrament, centuries before, when certain animals gave the reverence and respect to the Host which their owners had refused.

He turned to Rua. "In fifty years' time it will be the centenary of the miracle. I'd like you to have the pamphlet I've written reprinted."

"Fifty years, Don Bosco, 1903! Oh, I am afraid long before then death will have dealt me a low trick!"

"Death will not have dealt you any kind of trick, low or lovely. You'll be here; remember what I've asked you." (He did.)

When the holidays started, Michael Rua went with Don Bosco, Margaret and twenty-six boys, to walk to the Becchi and stay on Joseph's farm. On the way, Don Bosco said to the boy, "On October 3rd, it will be the feast of Our Lady of the Rosary. The parish priest will come to Becchi and I'll ask him to formally clothe you with the clerical cassock. All right?" "All right." Michael took the opportunity when they were alone to ask, "You remember when we first met and you were giving out medals, there were none left for me but you made as if to cut your hand in half. What did you mean?"

"Why, Michael, it means that you and I will from now on share everything: the work, the problems, the debts, the responsibilities. You will be like the Israelites, having a lot to suffer; you will have to cross the Red Sea, go through the desert and the wilderness; but you will see great things done for God, when you get to the promised land, and at the end of it all, we shall be together for ever, in Heaven. Now you know."

Chapter Twenty-Three

WE SHALL CALL OURSELVES SALESIANS

THE NUMBER OF students went on increasing, thirty-five in 1854, eventually 121 in 1857. The problem was to find 'sheep becoming shepherds' to look after them. One day Don Bosco called yet another four boys to his room: Rua already knew what to expect but listened with the others: "You boys know that Don Bosco (he usually spoke of himself in the third person) does what he can for all of you but he is alone. If you will give me a hand, I tell you that thousands of boys are waiting for us; Our Lady will send us great oratories, schools, workshops, churches, many priests who will help . . . and not only in Italy but in Europe, America . . . . Our Lady wants us to form a society, to help realise all this work."

The boys looked at him astounded. That night in a notebook Michael Rua recorded what happened: "Four of us, Rocchielli, Artiglia, Cagliero and Rua proposed, with the help of God and in the spirit of St. Francis of Sales, to make a practical exercise of charity towards our neighbour. To implement this proposal, we shall all make a promise, and if possible, later make a vow to the Lord; all who do this now or in the future, will call themselves Salesians."

It should be stressed that this 'society' was understood only to be a group promising to help Don Bosco in his work; at this stage there was no question of forming a religious order or congregation. In Don Bosco's mind, it was however, a first step towards that aim.

The Rose Walk

Many worthy men and women still, of course, looked upon Don Bosco as a visionary, a little unbalanced; some others saw his ability to build and to expand as having some secret banker; it seemed all too easy. Some years later, talking to some of his early Salesians in 1864, he spoke of this, telling them of an early dream, in 1847, when Our Lady showed him an enchanting garden, through which was a rose walk, a covered portico, entirely of beautiful roses, even the path through it. She first suggested he take his shoes off, which he gladly did as he did not want to crush the flowers, but after the first steps realised that the roses hid sharp thorns and he went back. "You see," said Our Lady, "you need good strong shoes to walk this path." Others joined him for a while but most of them left him, saying, "We have been deceived". As he pushed on through, he was lacerated on every side and soon bleeding. Then a group came from the other end and they went through together, all sadly hurt; but at the end, their wounds were healed. Our Lady told him, "You will have to go through many trials and need the strong shoes of mortification; but if you persevere, you will truly enter into a garden of roses without thorns". "But," added Don Bosco, "while we were pushing our way through, we could hear people saying, 'How fortunate Don Bosco is, walking through roses!' They could not see the hidden thorns."

A Valuable Recruit

Don Alasonatti was a teacher-priest, three years older than Don Bosco. They were good friends and Don Bosco used to tease him. "Why, look, you have thirty boys to look after, I've hundreds! Come along and help!"

"What wages will you pay me?"

"Bread, work and heaven at the end. But you'll be able to store up some sleep for the future."

They joked but Don Alasonatti began to think seriously. He was a serious minded teacher, a touch demanding of obedience at times but generally well liked by the boys. In 1854, he made up his mind when a brief letter arrived from Don Bosco, "Come and help me to say my breviary". Shortly after, he presented himself at the door of Don Bosco's room, with a bag and with his breviary under his arm. "Tell me where I can go to say my breviary."

"Come; I'll take you to what we'll call the bursar's office; you can do the books, use your arithmetical skill; this will be your kingdom."

"All right. Just tell me what you want and I'll carry out, as best I can, all your ideas, even if sometimes I don't agree. Heaven has to be won!"

He was to prove an immense help to Don Bosco and the Oratory, taking a great weight of worry and business off his friend's shoulders. But his first duty as a priest, the next day, was to go on a sick call to a man suffering from cholera.

Death Stalks the Streets of Borgo Dora

Cholera came to Turin at the end of that July, 1854. The Court fled to the castle of Caselette. The epicentre of the pestilence was around the slums of

Borgo Dora, where the undernourished immigrants offered little resistance to the attacks. Eight hundred fell victims, five hundred died, in the first month. The mayor appealed to the courageous to help; in an atmosphere of death in every street, it needed courage to help. On August 5th, Don Bosco spoke to the boys. "The mayor has asked for help. Many of you are too young but some of the bigger boys could help. I know this disease is contagious but I promise you that if you keep in the grace of God and avoid all mortal sin, you will not contract it. If any of you feel you could come with me to the hospitals or to people's houses to find out the sick, it will be a good work that God will bless. Think it over."

That evening fourteen boys put their names on the list, a few days later there were thirty, some of them quite young. Don Bosco divided them into three groups, the oldest to help in the actual care of the victims in the hospitals, a second group to go round the houses looking for stricken families, and a third group, the youngest, to hold themselves ready to run any errand, take any messages. It was hard and unpleasant work. Don Bosco insisted on taking all precautions, carrying out the instructions of the doctors. The boys were heroic; Margaret too, was their ready helper. When she had no more linen to give and yet another boy was in the kitchen begging for something to cover a sick woman, she got out the last spare altar cloth. "I am sure Our Lord won't mind." The wedding dress had long ago been sold. None of the boys fell sick of the cholera. By the end of November, the plague ended, with 1,400 dead in the city.

Bronze Giants with Sad Faces

Sixteen year old Giovanni Cagliero returned from a hospital feeling ill, probably from eating bad fruit. The doctor diagnosed not cholera but typhus. The fever lasted through September without improvement; his condition worsened and two doctors, called in for consultation, could only shake their heads. They advised that the boy should be given the Last Sacraments. Don Bosco was so upset that he could only ask Giuseppe Buzzetti to break the news of this gently to Cagliero while he went to the chapel. When he got back to the sick room and was walking to the bed, he stopped, looked fixedly at something over the bed, and, then after a few seconds, smiled.

"Is this my last confession? Am I going to die, Don Bosco?" the boy said in a weak voice.

"No, Giovani," replied Don Bosco, "you are not going to die; you are going to get better, to become a priest, to do a great deal of work, far, far

The house of the Becchi, home of John Bosco's childhood, now preserved as it was.

Don Bosco's Mamma Margaret, from a drawing.
She died in 1856, after mothering Don Bosco's boys at Valdocco for ten years.

The Moglia farm where young John Bosco spent nearly three happy years.

An artist's conception of Don Cafasso, now St Joseph Cafasso, Don Bosco's dearest friend and guide.

The Pinardi House, restored and enlarged with the Oratory well established. It has now been demolished, with a small chapel on the site.

How Don Bosco heard confessions outside before Pinardi. The boy was Paul Albera, his second successor.

1870 group of Salesian priests and clerics with Don Bosco, seen here to be short of stature. Future missionaries, Don Costamagna and Don Cagliero, on left, marked with a cross.

This photograph of 1861 is of great historical interest. The boy in the left foreground is wearing one of the military coats and caps procured by Don Bosco: several others can be made out. The small boy in front of Don Bosco is apparently holding on to his brother, one of the quite young seminarians given shelter by the Saint when the diocesan seminary was closed. Others can be seen wearing birettas and cassocks.

Satirical cartoon of the 'miracle worker' don Bosco (Dominus Lingus = Bosco = Wood) who has been fabricating 'enemies of Italy' in his priest factory, and suggesting the sooner he emigrates to America the better!

Canonisation painting of M. Mary Mazzarello Rome, June 24th 1951. With St John Bosco, she founded the Salesian Sisters, the Daughters of Mary Help of Christians, in 1872. She died only nine years later, after founding 25 Houses, convents, orphanages, hostels, etc.

The only extant photograph of Saint Mary D. Mazzarello, centre front row, with departing second missionary expedition, 1877.

Ascetical Blessed Michael Rua, who shared everything with Don Bosco, was the first Salesian, the first Successor, a great force in establishing the Salesians in the Anglo-Irish Province. He died in 1910. He visited England three times.

Dominic Savio, the Boy saint, flower of Don Bosco's work, died before his fifteenth birthday, canonised 1954.

'A Salesian House without music is dead!' said Don Bosco, seen sitting on a raised chair. On his right is the bearded one and only Guiseppe Buzzetti, next to him the youthful Don Cagliero, master of music.

The first missionary expedition, 1875. Don Bosco is handing the Salesian Rule book to Don Cagliero, leader of the group. The military gentleman is the Argentinian Consul.

Barcelona 1886. Don Rua is bending over the ailing Don Bosco. The white face of the lady between the two boys over the bearded priest is that of Doña Dorotea de Chopitea, 'Mother of the Salesians in Spain', now 'Venerable'.

Front row centre: Don Paul Albera second successor of Don Bosco. On his left, legs crossed, the inimitable Bro. Pietro Enria.

Cardinal John Cagliero, first Salesian Bishop and Cardinal.

Top: Don Philip Rinaldi, the reluctant boy who became the third Salesian Rector Major.

Bottom left: Pope Pius IX, the 'priest who loved humanity', Don Bosco's good friend and supporter.

Bottom Right: Pope Leo XIII, comfort and support of Don Bosco's declining years.

Top: Father Charles Macey, young English convert, who took over from Father McKiernan and was the founder of Salesian work in the English-speaking world; under the practical assistance and encouragement of Don Rua, he built schools and churches in Battersea, Burwash, Chertsey, Farnborough, initiated Salesian work in Malta and South Africa and introduced to England the first Salesian Sisters.

Bottom: Father Edward McKiernan, the young Irish priest sent by Don Bosco, November 1887, to head the English foundation. Sadly he died scarcely a year later, aged only 27.

Don Bosco, old and infirm, in Barcelona 1886.

away . . ." and with that left the room without more ado. Cagliero did indeed soon got better and left for his home in Castelnuovo for a long convalescence. Some time later on his return to Turin, he and Buzzetti asked Don Bosco what had happened.

"Well, when I got to the door, I was going across to your bed when I saw a bright light; over your head was a shining white dove, carrying an olive branch which it slowly dropped over your forehead. Then the scene changed, into wide spaces, then round your bed I saw gigantic figures, men with bronze skin, tattooed in red paint, looking sad and anxiously whispering, 'If he dies, who will come to help us?' It all vanished in seconds; but I knew you would get better and there was no need for the Last Sacraments."

Chapter Twenty-Four

THE BOY WHO WAS MADE OF GOOD STUFF

THE CURATE AT Mondonio was a fellow student of Don Bosco's, a Don Cugliero, who came to him one day, to say, "I hear you have amongst those street arabs of yours in Turin, some boys who seem to have signs of a vocation. Well, I've a little lad here, his name is Dominic Savio, who is another Saint Aloysius Gonzaga in my opinion!"

"Another exaggeration! Well, I'll be here a couple of days; ask the father to bring the lad along and we'll have a chat."

Domenico Savio, Dominic in English, was twelve, born in 1842, his father a blacksmith. His first interview with Don Bosco so impressed the priest that he recorded it later almost verbatim. "For candour and intelligence, here was no exaggeration. I was amazed," wrote Don Bosco, "at what I saw, how the power of grace had already wrought marvels in this soul, still so young in years." He gave him the memory test, beloved of Italians of that age, a page to learn a day, which Dominic brought him back word perfect within minutes.

"I see you are made of good stuff, Dominic."

"What can this stuff be used for, Father?"

"To make a fine garment for the Lord."

"Well, if I am the stuff and you are the tailor, perhaps we can both together make this fine garment."

"Well, you can come with me to Turin and start Latin; and then what?"

"Then, Father, if it's God's will, I should hope to become a priest."

When on October 29th, Dominic arrived at the Oratory he saw over Don Bosco's desk a card with the words, *Da mihi animas, coetera tolle.* He asked what they meant and the priest explained, literally, "Give me souls, take away the rest"; in other words, all we are interested in here is the spiritual good of people; riches, power, glory, these things don't matter and we don't look for them. These five Latin words were the mainspring of Don Bosco's apostolate from the first.

Dominic remarked, "I see, here we are not in the business of making money, but in saving souls. I hope I will be able to take part in this business".

The next day he was off with Michael Rua and the rest to Don Bonzanino's school, possibly wearing one of the shabby army coats like the others. "From that day," wrote Don Bosco later, "he fulfilled even the least duty in a manner no-one could ever surpass."

World Joy, Balloons and Processions

December 8th, 1854, was an historic day for the Catholic world. It was the Feast of the Immaculate Conception and Pope Pius IX chose the day to proclaim, in St. Peter's Rome, in the presence of a vast congregation of prelates and people, that it was of faith that, from the first moment of her existence, that is, from the moment of her conception, Mary the Mother of God had never been subject to original sin. The Pope was simply confirming what had been the belief of the Church for centuries. Four years later, at Lourdes, Mary herself declared to the child Bernadette, who asked for her name: "I am the Immaculate Conception." To those who might question this manner of giving a name, one could reply that it seems to run in the family, since her Son, Jesus declared, "I am the Resurrection and the Life".

But the world that day was not concerned with linguistic niceties. For a while Italy, with its traditional love for the Madonna, forgot its troubles and gave everywhere expression to its joy and pride. All along the river that flows through Turin there were lights and altars, thousands of coloured balloons were released and as night fell, a great procession went to pay the homage and devotion of the people of Turin at the church of the Consolata, the ancient Marian shrine. Proudly and happily in that procession was Don Bosco leading his boys, singing and praising God in honour of Her to whom had been shown great marvels.

Cholera Orphans

A Last memory of that intense year of 1854 for Don Bosco was a result of the cholera outbreak. Many children had been left orphans and the mayor of the city appealed to charitable people to take care of some of them. Although he had not an inch to spare, Don Bosco accepted twenty. One of them was a boy called Pietro Enria. He remembered that when the little group arrived at Valdocco, there were no beds for any of them; for the first few nights he and the others slept on a bag of leaves. Many of these children were very young and Don Bosco found time to teach them the elements of reading and writing. "More than that!" said Pietro, "I had only the clothes I was wearing and I remember I had to stay in bed so that Don Bosco and his mother could mend and patch my jacket and pants."

Pietro Enria was another lifelong dweller at Valdocco. He became an infirmarian and attended Don Bosco in his last illness; he it was who closed the Saint's eyes in death.

Chapter Twenty-Five

AWAY WITH THE MONKS! DEATHS AT COURT

AT THE END of the year of 1854, the two Houses of the Piedmont Parliament were asked to consider a law which would suppress the 'useless' religious Houses, under the pretext of helping the poorer parishes. 'Useless' would be those Houses, monasteries and convents whose members did not either teach, care for the sick or for the orphans. The Bill was to be debated in the Spring. If both Houses passed it, the king had the deciding vote.

On a freezing day in December, Don Bosco called his helpers to his room to tell them of a vivid dream he had had that night, of a Court herald, proclaiming, "Great funeral at Court!" He told them he had written to the king, Victor Emmanuel II and told him of the dream. Five days later the dream was repeated, but this time the herald was crying, "Great funerals at Court!" this time in the plural. At dawn, he wrote again to the king, who, it was reported, was furious.

Royal Funerals

On January 12th, the Queen Mother Maria Teresa died and was buried on the 15th; she was fifty-four. On January 8th, the Queen, Maria Adelaide, had given birth to a son but did not rally. She was given the Last Sacraments on the 20th, and died later in the day. She was thirty-three. The king's brother, Ferdinand of Savoy, fell ill at the same time and died on February 11th. He was thirty-three.

The Law of Suppression was passed in both the Camera (Commons) and the Senate. The king delayed; but on May 29th he signed. The law was immediately put into execution and according to the official biography, we are told that 334 religious houses were closed and 5,456 members of their communities sent away. The Pope excommunicated all those responsible. Meanwhile, the son born to the dead Queen in January, died on May 17th, the king's only son. When the facts of the two dreams became known, there were many frightened people in high places in Turin.

The First Salesian

Meanwhile life had to go on. Several times in his weekly talks to his growing number of clerics Don Bosco had spoken briefly of the value of the virtues of poverty, chastity and obedience, without elaborating. On the feast of the Annunciation, March 25th, 1855, he put the question to Michael Rua. "Michael, do you feel like making the simple vows of poverty, chastity and obedience for three years?" Michael readily acquiesced; he was quite ready to give three years of his life to help Don Bosco, which was all that this implied. It was the simplest ceremony. Don Bosco stood by his side as Rua kneeling before the crucifix, murmured: "I make a vow to God to be poor, chaste and obedient for three years and to put myself in the hands of Don Bosco . . . ." There was no witness; but it could be held that this was the real beginning of the Salesian Congregation, Don Bosco its founder, Michael Rua its first member.

He and all the other clerics had an appalling work load by any standards; they would be teaching religion, taking the refectory, out in the recreations, looking after the workshops; and all the time, using every spare moment to study for the State examinations.

Sunday, far from being a day of rest, was a day of unremitting activity. There were now three oratories in being, each of them looked after by a priest friend of Don Bosco; but when one priest could no longer undertake the work, Don Bosco appointed the seventeen year old Michael Rua to take his place. Michael would be there early in the morning to clean up and prepare the chapel. He would arrange for the confessions when a priest came, see to the Mass, and after the Mass 'do Don Bosco' for the rest of the day, with all that exhausting idea implied. When the last prayers had been said, a few of the boys would accompany him home through the gas-lit streets. A feature of his 'Guardian Angel' Oratory was that the boys were almost all chimneysweepers, tiny fellows most of them who used to descend upon the city in the autumn crying their trade through the streets, expecting the householders to come out and get them to clean their chimneys in preparation for the winter. It was an appalling trade even though many of them made light of it. They would go off cheerfully as they left him at the door, "See you Sunday, Michael!" Michael, completely exhausted, would find something left for him in the oven, probably also finding Cagliero, Anfossi and Francesia in from their own oratories. They would crawl up to their attic beds, sometimes too tired to get into bed, falling asleep on a chair. In the morning, the alarm would go at the inhuman hour of four o'clock; often, in Turin's hard winter, the water in their basins would be frozen (no heating, no running water!) and they would have to reach out for some snow, and rub their faces till they glowed! Then, with a blanket round their shoulders, to two hours study, before they got the boys up. Don Bosco has been accused of overworking his young men to 'an early grave'. On the face of it, there is no point in killing off your best helpers, defeating your own object. Certainly the work was hard; certainly these first helpers were of a special breed. As for an early grave, Don Rua, who 'did three men's work,' died at seventy-three, Cagliero died at eighty-eight, and Francesia at ninety-two!

Tête-à-tête with the Minister, Prison Outing

Urban Rattazzi was the Minister of the Interior and one of the authors of the infamous bill for the suppression of 'useless Orders'. He was a pragmatic man but thought a good deal of Don Bosco. "Here is a man who works for the poor, who does a worthwhile job." (Incidentally saving the Government a heap of troubles with the sons of those same poor, its abandoned youth.) Don Bosco always had ready access to him.

In 1845, a new prison for young offenders was opened in Turin, called the Generala. Most of the boys were there for petty thefts or because their parents could not control them. Don Bosco was a frequent visitor and got to know them well. In the summer of 1855 he gave them a three day retreat, at which almost all went to confession and were in high spirits. So impressed was the priest that he went to the director with a proposal that filled that worthy man with horror. "My dear padre, you must be out of your mind! Take these young rascals for a day in the country? Certainly not! Only the Minister . . . ." So off to the Minister, Urban Rattazzi. The Minister listened and thought a while. "All right; you can have them. We'll arrange for a suitable number of men, in plain clothes, along the roads . . . ."

"No, Minister, no-one; that's part of it. No guards!"

"Come on, Don Bosco! Why, not one will come back with you!"

"On the contrary, not one will be missing. I give you my word. If one is missing, well, you can put me in prison in his place!"

They both laughed at that. "All right. Have it your way; I'll trust you."

Back at the Generala with the news. Shouts to bring the roof down!

"All right now. We'll have all day. There'll be no guards, either in uniform or in plain clothes. But I've given my word; no-one is to try to clear off. If even one is missing, I'll be disgraced, will never be allowed to come here again. I've given *my* word; now what about your word?" There was a pause while some of them got together. "There will be no clearing off, for anyone; you have our word, Don Bosco," and the bigger boys looked round meaningfully. They had a grand day, with the food packed on a donkey, Mass in the country, games and fun and bits of prizes; and on the way home, Don Bosco himself on the donkey, tired but supremely happy. The suspicious director met them and had them counted, three hundred of them. All present and correct; and the Minister was as happy as any one. He had probably won a good bet!

Chapter Twenty-Six

REASON, RELIGION AND LOVING KINDNESS

"WHY CAN'T WE get the same results that you do, Don Bosco?" asked the Minister Rattazzi after the Generala success.

"You have to get results through threats and punishments; we see our boys as given to us by God to care for, we try to treat them with reason, through the exercise of their religion and through kindness. As priests we would have a moral force that you could not understand."

For years Don Bosco was asked to explain his system, "I have no system," he would repeat, "I just go along and cope with things as they arise". He would try to show these boys, the good and the not so good, that he loved them as Jesus Christ would love them. And to his Salesians he would say, "It is not enough that the boys should be loved, they must know they are loved."

In the Rule book that Don Bosco drew up for the Salesians, he added, in response to requests, an appendix about his system. This was written about 1876. He began by saying there were two systems in use. One he called the 'repressive system' in which laws and rules of discipline are made known to the pupils, as in the army and prisons; they are warned that if they do not observe these rules, they will be punished.

His system he called the 'Preventive system, sistemo preventivo'. This is not as easily translated as it may seem. A preventive move in war is to get there before the enemy! Prevention is certainly better than cure. Let the boys know what is expected of them but help them to keep these rules for their own good, help them, with reason, to understand. Watch over them like good fathers and brothers who will prevent the little children from falling into the fire, or over cliffs. If you want to be respected, respect your pupils. Never humiliate them in any way; if reproofs have to be made, let them be made in private, not in public; and then forgotten. Harsh punishment should never be used; a favour withdrawn, a privilege forfeited, are often, if not always far more effective than corporal punishment.

In 1876, it was thirty years since the Oratory days of the 1840's when the only rule Don Bosco gave to his boys was to sing, run, jump, shout, make as much row as you like only as long as you do not offend God. Thirty years later, dealing now with colleges, boarding schools with fee paying students, his Salesian schools had to follow the standard disciplines, many of them laid down by the State. In the schools of today, we are witnessing the gradual disappearance of boarding schools in favour of day-schools where, outside classtimes, there is often little contact between teachers and pupils; brief 'dinner hour' recreations give little opportunity for getting to know one another as human beings. School activities, sports, games, hikes, theatricals, youth clubs, offer some help but do not cover all the school. Apart from his Sunday oratories, Don Bosco's first schools meant that he and his early helpers were with the boys twenty-four hours a day. Circumstances are very different today.

Salesian analysts studying Don Bosco's 'system' consider it more clearly illustrated in a long, dialogue 'dream' recounted in detail by the priest in 1884. Then, approaching his seventieth year, he was taken in a nostalgic visit back to the oratory life of the '40's, to its happy, ideal relationships with the boys. The dream is meant for the Salesians; he waves an admonitory finger at those in the schools of the 1880's. In the early days 'we were boys with the boys, joining them in their games, taking part with them in everything'. Then, "the Salesians played with the boys, now, in 1884, they merely supervise them". Don Bosco and those who took part in the dialogue (mainly our old friend Giuseppe Buzzetti!) were almost exclusively concerned with the recreations. But this, too, was 100 years ago.

Today's Salesians, especially those who have to try to bring a Salesian 'charism' into day-schools, many mixed, with their limited opportunities, have obvious problems. One can only say that they are conscious of these problems and do their best to meet them, that many of our young and enthusiastic Salesians (and some not so young) can compare very favourably with the dedicated young Italians who laid the foundations of the world-wide Salesian Society, in St. John Bosco's day.

None of us can hope to approach Don Bosco himself. It must be remembered that God gave him a special mission; to carry this out, he was also given great spiritual and natural gifts. To the spiritual gifts and graces God gave him, he corresponded to an heroic degree. His life of prayer, of work, of suffering supported his complete commitment; he gave everything: all his time, all his endeavours, all his hopes, all his love; he was indeed a great saint. In a century of great men and women, he was one of the greatest. (For the historically minded, it is interesting to compare the *private* lives of certain other 'great' figures of the century with those of such as Don

Bosco: history's values can be false indeed.) True, he was not God. He was human; humanum est errare. He could make mistakes, mistakes he would acknowledge, being the saint he was. He could weep at the end of his life for the opportunities missed, for his failures. We would not call them failures.

Chapter Twenty-Seven

GOOD-BYE TO A BOY AND TO A MOTHER

ON THE FIRST Sunday of April, 1855, Don Bosco preached a sermon on 'Becoming a Saint,' which probably had little effect on the majority; but one boy took it to heart. On the feast of St. John the Baptist, June 24th, Don Bosco's 'name day,' he suggested to the boys that if they sent him a little note asking for something, he would do his best to get it for them. There were bizarre requests, one bright youth asking for enough nougat to keep him for a year! Dominic Savio, the boy who had listened to the sermon, put five words on a scrap of paper: "Help me become a saint". Don Bosco called him. "For you, a boy, there are three ways to become holy. First, keep cheerful, no matter what happens or goes wrong. Second, carry out with perfect obedience all that you are asked to do, in your studies, your prayers, your daily tasks and duties. Thirdly, do good to others, help your companions even at the cost of some sacrifice. These are your steps to holiness."

Dominic took all this to heart. He was popular with his companions, though some would make snide remarks about his 'piety'. Not that that worried him as one boy found out when he brought into the playground a paper with unsuitable pictures. Dominic walked up to the group round him, snatched the paper and tore it into shreds. "This is not the place for this sort of thing; here we have a priest doing everything for us and you bring in this muck!"

Dominic believed in putting his best into everything he did. Found in recent years, an old companion's recollection of him describes him as a fierce battler in games, in spite of his slight frame. However, as the harsh winter of 1856 set in, Don Bosco noticed him looking rather pale and drawn. "Going out to school in all weathers is not doing you any good, Dominic. You'd better stay in and go to Don Francesia's class. You won't have to get up so early. Good health is a gift of God and we must take care of it."

Sodality of Mary Immaculate

Thinking about 'making yourself holy by helping others' Dominic consulted a few special friends and asked them about forming a sort of 'secret Society,' (beloved by boys!) not to blow anyone up, but to give unobtrusive help to any who might need it. Don Bosco thought it might work but counselled time to think about it. Eventually a brief 'Rule' was drawn up, chiefly by the 14 year old Savio, by which members of the group, calling themselves the 'Sodality of Mary Immaculate' would act as unknown 'guardian angels' to designated boys in need of help, especially new boys, helping them to get used to school ways, to make friends, to join in games and other activities. In these and in other ways, the group had to be 'little apostles,' doing Don Bosco's work (and God's) among their companions.

One day, the cleric in charge of the refectory noticed that Dominic, as Lent began, was depriving himself of necessary food. He spoke about it to Don Bosco who sent for the boy.

"Look, Dominic, the first rule about becoming holy is to obey. I hear you are doing too much fasting and what's more, even putting stones in your bed and sleeping in this cold weather with only one blanket on your bed. Now I forbid you to do anything of the sort without my express permission. I assure you that your obedience will gain you far more grace than those penances which are damaging your health." Dominic was a little distressed that he had been found out but, of course, at once obeyed.

The Boy who Talked with God

From the first meeting Don Bosco had been astonished how far this boy had progressed in genuine piety and knowledge of the things of God. Evidence of this began to show itself in various ways. One day, missing at meals, Dominic was found in the church of St. Francis de Sales in a state of ecstasy. He had been there three hours: he thought it had been only minutes.

Already that winter there had been another mysterious occurrence. One night, when Don Bosco was working late, a knock at the door brought in Dominic (who ought to have been hours in bed!). "Don Bosco, please come with me. You are needed." After some hesitation, Don Bosco put on his coat and followed the boy, taking with him the essentials for the Last Sacraments. They went through the dim, gas-lit streets and dark alleys until Dominic stopped outside a house. "Here you are needed." Don Bosco knocked at the door. A woman peered out. "Oh, a priest! Who sent you? My husband is at the point of death. He gave up his religion some time ago but is now crying for a priest to hear his confession and put him right with God. Oh, come, please hurry!"

As they went back, Don Bosco was left pondering how Dominic could possibly have known about the man and how, indeed, a boy from the country who rarely left the Oratory, could possibly find his way at night through the city streets. Much the same thing happened a little later. This time, Dominic led the priest to a larger house where the owners declared there was no-one sick or in any way in need of a priest. Dominic quietly insisted. "Well," said the man, probably a little amused, "come in and look through the house yourselves. I assure you, you will not find anyone." As they left the last bedroom without finding anyone, Dominic said, "There is still the attic". And there, in the attic, lying on some sacks, was a woman, obviously near to death. The owner exclaimed, "Why, she's one of our cleaners! We thought she'd left hours ago!" When they got back to Valdocco, Don Bosco asked Dominic how he had known these things. The boy looked confused, said nothing and then began to cry. Don Bosco dared not question him further but it was plainly evident that in this Valdocco Oratory there was a boy who talked with God.

In 1850, Pope Pius IX had restored the Hierarchy in England. It was the time of the 'Second Spring' in that country and there were great hopes in Europe that it could return to the Faith it had lost three centuries before. Don Bosco was well aware of developments and used to ask his clerics and the boys to pray and sometimes to offer their Holy Communions for the conversion of England, a country growing in importance and power in the world. Dominic himself would offer his Communion for this intention on Saturdays. One day he told Don Bosco a dream he had had.

"I found myself walking in a country covered with mist, when I saw Pope Pius carrying a torch. A voice said, 'This is England, for which land God is preparing great triumphs'. When you see the Holy Father in Rome, please will you tell him about this dream?" Don Bosco promised that he would.

But now, in this February of 1857, Dominic was plainly ill, weak with incessant coughing. The doctor advised that he should return home, stopping all studies, at least for a couple of months.

Dominic accepted the verdict, though with some reluctance; he would have preferred to stay at the Oratory with Don Bosco and his friends.

"But," said Don Bosco, "you are only going home for a while until you get stronger and then you can come back."

"No, Don Bosco, I shall not be coming back," he said quietly. His father came to fetch him. As they said good-bye, Dominic reminded Don Bosco of his promise to tell the Holy Father about his dream of England. (Don Bosco kept his promise the following year.)

Dominic died on March 9th, 1857, still more than three weeks short of his fifteenth birthday. The Church pondered long and hard about this remarkable boy, but eventually, almost a hundred years later, declared he was heroic in virtue and on June 12th, 1954, he was canonised, Saint Dominic Savio, the youngest canonised saint in history. (There were martyrs in the first centuries, canonised later by popular acclaim, who might have been as young or even younger. Not that it matters in the least: they are all in Heaven, very dear children of God!)

Nine years later, Don Bosco and Dominic met again in one of the more famous of his 'dreams,' one that covers ten pages in the official biography. The priest found himself in a place of 'marvellously beautiful light'. To the sound of music, he saw Dominic, splendidly arrayed, leading a large group of boys and Salesians. He could only stammer, "Dominic! But where are we, you and all these?" "We are in a place of happiness," was the reply and Dominic went on to discuss the work and progress of the Salesians, saying that they would do great good if they were faithful to their vows and their devotion to God and to Our Lady, the Mother of God.

"As for you, dear Don Bosco, you have still much to endure before you, too, come to be with us in this place of such happiness."

Farewell to the Mother

'Mamma Margaret' had spent ten years with her son, coping with an ever increasing household of boys for whom the first port of call in all their needs was her kitchen. She had hoped to spend those ten years on her son Joseph's farm, surrounded by her many grandchildren: but God ruled otherwise. Now, in her quiet moments, she knew that 'the better part' had been allotted to her, The children of Valdocco were not hers, but she was their mother; for most of them, the only mother they had.

In November 1856 she fell ill; pneumonia was diagnosed, in those days almost always fatal, especially for those worn out with work and years. Don Borel gave her the last Sacraments; Joseph and the older children came from the Becchi. Don Bosco was grief stricken, not only because he was losing a wonderful mother but because it was he who had imposed upon her such crushing burdens. Now she was dying. But dying though she was, Margaret remained her practical self. "John, you are making me feel worse, seeing you suffer so. You are exhausted. Please, go to your room and rest. I know you will never forget me. Go now, my son, go and God will bless you."

About three in the morning, Joseph came to tell him that it was all over. Two hours later, he roused his friend Giuseppe Buzzetti and they went to offer the first of many Requiem Masses at his mother's favourite church, the Consolata. She was sixty-eight. She was buried in her only presentable dress, in the pocket of which they found the coin Don Bosco had given her some time before to replace her ancient, quite deplorable hat.

Shortly afterwards Michael Rua went home. "Mother, you know that now Mamma Margaret has gone, we have no-one to make the soup and darn our socks. Won't you come?" Giovanna Maria Rua went to the Oratory with great heart, aged fifty-six, and stayed there twenty heroic years, to Don Bosco's immense relief.

Chapter Twenty-Eight

MONK OR NO MONK, I STAY WITH DON BOSCO!

THE MINISTER URBAN Rattazzi saw Don Bosco again in the summer of 1857. After the cholera and the success of the Generala, he was feeling kindly about the 'oratories'.

"They ought to carry on, Don Bosco; I hope you'll have many more years yet but even you can't live for ever. When you go, who is going to carry on? I think you should train some of your young helpers in your methods and your ideas and let them carry on."

Don Bosco smiled, "You know, what you are asking me to do is to found a new religious order! That coming from you who only two years ago supported the closing of 300 monasteries! The State would shut me, too!"

The Minister smiled back, "I know all about these monasteries but if they make themselves independent of the State, then they should be closed. No, Don Bosco, if you or anyone were to form an association of men who would observe the laws of the State, would pay its taxes, would retain its own rights, that is, its members would retain their property and be subject to the State, then no-one could touch you . . . . You would be a group of free citizens; if your association were to have as its object religious ends such as yours, that would make no difference at all."

They parted in friendly fashion and Don Bosco went away pondering over the Minister's views. The State would accept what he already had in mind; would the Church accept?

Meanwhile he would push on slowly with his recruiting of the "sheep who would become shepherds". After Rua, Don Alasonatti and Francesia took the three year temporary vows, again 'only to give Don Bosco a hand' for the time. But he began to make other preparations. Using his experience in the Oratory and later in his schools and workshops, he began to draw up a series of Rules. He sent a draft copy to his Archbishop, who was still in exile. Mgr. Fransoni replied with an encouraging letter and comment but suggested that he go down to Rome and consult the Pope (who had by now returned to the city). So Michael Rua was instructed to draw up in his best script the draft 'Rules and Constitutions'. "Copy them well, Michael, and you and I will take them down to Rome." They had to get passports to go to the Papal States and the journey was arduous but on March 9th, 1858, Don Bosco had his first audience with Pope Pius IX, who received him with a kindness and understanding that he never retracted. He took the manuscript with him to study it and give his views. On March 21st, they met again. This time, the Pope spoke well of the proposed Rule which he felt would do much good if exercised on behalf of youth, continuing Don Bosco's work. "It is mild in concept and not too demanding. I suggest you call it a Society rather than a Congregation, and ensure that each member is in the face of the Church a religious, and in the face of the State, a free citizen."

Don Bosco reflected to himself that the views of the Pope and the Minister were remarkably alike.

When Pius IX saw Don Bosco for the third time, he told him to experiment with the Rules for a while and meanwhile to give a copy to a Cardinal Gaudi who would study them from every point of view. So Michael Rua had another job; before they left, on this occasion Don Bosco introduced his young assistant to the Pope and also told him of Dominic Savio's dream of the Pope in England, as he had promised. Pius IX, very pleased, saw it as confirmation of his restoring the English hierarchy in 1850.

A Week to Decide a Life

The next step took much more than a year to decide. Don Bosco had many helpers at Valdocco including seminarians to whom he had given the clerical habit; but they were destined not for him but for the diocese, to go to other seminaries eventually while the Turin seminary remained closed. Only his own helpers were his and on December 9th, 1859, he called them to his room. There were nineteen of them. He spoke of his decision to found a new religious Society; vows would be temporary and then perpetual, a commitment for life. They were already 'Salesians' in name; if they joined the Society, they would be Salesians in reality. He asked them to go away, and pray, and think about the step.

The lying propaganda against the older 'useless' Orders had had some effect; 'monks' were not popular; the ebullient Giovanni Cagliero debated long with himself: a life's commitment, here? But then he burst out, "Monk or no monk, I'm going to stick by Don Bosco!" It became a famous saying. The crucial meeting was on December 18th. Seventeen were there, all of whom signed the document creating themselves the "Society of St. Francis de Sales". By unanimous consent, Don Bosco was elected as the Superior General; other offices were voted for. Don Alasonatti was the only priest and most of the office-holders were teenagers, or nearly so. Boys almost they were, who began this unusual new religious Society, a defect, however, that time would remedy (as Don Bosco drily pointed out to certain venerable objectors!). Now the Salesians were born, legally!

Crisis for Giuseppe Buzzetti

One famous name was missing from that gathering. Giuseppe Buzzetti had a pistol, which going off when it should not have done, robbed him of a finger. By the rules of those days, that meant he could not be accepted for the priesthood, so he abandoned his studies. He was a large young man, a giant some called him, and a frequent bodyguard to Don Bosco (which probably had more effect on the Saint's safety than we know). He had been in the early days Don Bosco's right hand, taking on every job that was going. Now he saw no prospect before him. Family pressure upset him: "You are wasting your time". He became depressed, decided to pack it all up, went out and got a job and then came to tell Don Bosco.

"You know, Don Bosco, what we have done all these years. Now I'm nothing; these young clerics I taught as boys, taught some of them how to wipe their noses, now are telling me what I have to do. It is too much; I've got a job and I am going . . . ."

Don Bosco, who could have said many things but in his widsom did not, replied quietly, "You have a job? I hope they're giving you good money? But you'll need something to start you off. Here's the key of the cash box. I don't know what there is in it but there is something. Take what you want and if there isn't enough for your needs just let me know, and I'll get what you want. We have always been good friends, Giuseppe, and I know you will not forget me." Whereupon poor Buzzetti could no longer keep it up; he burst into tears, gave the key back and cried, "No, no, I can't leave you, Don Bosco, and never shall, ever!"

The Brothers

"Religious in shirt sleeves," Don Bosco called them, these Salesian Brothers, or 'Coadjutors'. We shall see some of them later but from the first his idea of them was that they should be as fully Salesian as priests. As the priests, he gave them no distinguishing habit; the priests should dress like the diocesan clergy, the Brothers like every decent layman; and work in shirt-sleeves!' There is a wonderful tradition of Brothers around Don Bosco, some of them simple factotums, some like Giuseppe Buzzetti, craftsmasters, bursars, some professors, in recent years highly professional architects, composers, choirmasters, inventors of new processes in all sorts of arts and trades. Without the Brothers, the Salesian Society would be like a craftsman without an arm. And because they are religious, they have done, and are doing, untold good, mixing as they do easily among the boys and working people the world over. Some of them have died as martyrs, some led such heroic lives that their Cause for Beatification is being studied in Rome.

Chapter Twenty-Nine

STREET ARAB GENERAL

WITHIN A COUPLE of years of the death of Dominic Savio, Don Bosco had found time to write a 'Life' which became a best seller and still sells well today in many languages. But in the same year of Dominic's death, he met another boy of entirely different character whose 'life' he also in due time, felt constrained to write for his boys.

It was a chill, damp foggy evening in the autumn of 1857. Don Bosco was waiting for the Turin train on the platform of Carmagnola station. As he walked down some steps towards the dim lamplight, he saw a group of boys under it, playing cards, with one clear voice dominating all the others. From the bottom steps he jumped to their side, whereupon, the players, seeing through the murk this black figure on top of them, took to their heels and fled. All but one, who stood his ground, demanding, arms akimbo, "Who do you think you are, jumping on us like that?"

"Sorry to frighten you! Call them all back. But I'm Don Bosco. Who are you?"

"I'm Michael Magone. I'm thirteen and the general of my gang."

A distant whistle signalled the proximate arrival of the train. There was just time to find out that the boy's father was dead, the mother struggling to bring up the family and he himself, the eldest, having to exist on what he could pick up. The priest nevertheless felt that this boy, desperately poor though he was, a street arab, ripe for good or for evil depending upon who might influence him first, yet had personality and character.

"Look, Michael, take this medal to your Father Arricio and tell him that the priest who gave it to you here wants him to write to him in Turin, telling him all about you." Michael, much mollified, waved to him as the train moved off, obviously another conquest.

The letter from the good Father Arricio confirmed Michael's story as he had sketched it, adding that he proved too lively a character for the school, which threw him out, and although he went to Sunday school, he caused such upset that peace only reigned when he left, to everyone's relief. "Yet all this was due to his high spirits and boundless energy, and not to any malice.

Morally he was not a bad boy and if given a chance, could benefit by it. Perhaps Don Bosco could give him that chance?"

Don Bosco could and did and in due time Michael and his mother arrived at Valdocco. "Well, Michael are you going to turn us upside down, too?"

"Ah, no, Don Bosco, you'll see I'll fit in all right."

"Tell me, now, what do you want to do, to study or to learn a trade?"

"I'd like to study." (Surprising answer!)

"And if you do well at your studies, what then?"

"Well, then, if a rapscallion like me . . .," he laughed.

"If a rapscallion like you . . . ?"

"If a rapscallion like me could ever be good enough, I'd like to become a priest." (Even more surprising!)

He therefore went to the school. But let it be said, when the bell went for class, it was as if it was going for a funeral for Michael, so slowly did this reluctant schoolboy follow the others. But when the bell went for the end of class, out he burst like a rocket, tearing across the playground, leaping and shouting for sheer joy!

He was no plaster saint. The 'Sodality' put a steady boy on him to check him quietly when he used crude expressions and rough ways from his street arab days, which he would accept as quietly, and watch himself.

One day, to give him a little treat, Don Bosco took him out with him on an errand to the city. When they were passing through the market, a boy let out a string of oaths and blasphemies just beside them. Michael, without more ado, smacked him hard in the mouth. Within seconds they were at each other's throats, to the admiration of some of the bystanders. Don Bosco quickly pulled them apart, with Michael hissing at the other, "You can thank this priest for saving you; I'd have beaten you up good and proper. Watch your mouth next time!"

As they moved on, Don Bosco suggested that, while his zeal was praiseworthy, beating up the sinner wasn't perhaps the best way to stop bad language. (But before that 'dream', he would probably have done just that himself!)

Conscience Healed

At school, Michael quickly took the lead and was soon 'captain' of his team (or was he the general?). However, in one recreation, Don Bosco came across him sitting out the game by himself, obviously in low spirits.

"Come, Michael," he said, "I don't like to see you like this. Is there anything the matter? Aren't you well? Anything I can do?"

The boy hesitated, then said slowly.

"It's a matter of conscience, my conscience, I've a lot on it. When I see the other boys going to Communion, I feel bad."

"Well, you know you have only to go to one of the priests, just to make your confession and you'll feel a lot better."

Of course, it was to Don Bosco that Michael unburdened himself of his faults. Within minutes he was out on the playground, leading his team to victory. "Gosh, I feel grand now!"

It was not long after that when he came across a group in the playground near the gate; a boy was retailing some off-colour jokes to the others, some sniggering, some rather shamefaced but not leaving. Michael kept his fists to himself this time but went close to the storyteller, put his four fingers in his mouth and, inches from the other's ear, let fly a street urchin's whistle that nearly blew the fellow's head off! "Heigh, what do you think you're doing! Have you gone mad?" "No," said Michael, "It's you who've gone mad! Now shut up and be off with you!"

Seven Policemen for One Boy

Gradually his thoughts went more and more to that ultimate goal he had given himself, of the priesthood. He made for himself a list of seven things to notice, he called them 'seven policemen for one boy,' seven pointers to bring him nearer to God . . . frequent confession and communion, devotion to Our Lady, frequent prayer, invoking Jesus and Mary, keeping busy, no pampering of himself, keeping away from bad companions. The hand of Don Bosco is visible here for he had given similar lists to other boys.

On the last day of the year of 1859, Don Bosco gave a 'good night' talk gathering the boys about him under the porticos. He put his hand out and rested it on the head of the nearest boy; it was Michael's. The boys were to thank God for the past year and then ask Him to keep them in His grace through the year to come, "for someone of you may not be here this time next year".

Michael though as he went up to bed, "I wonder if that hand on my head means that I won't be here next year?"

In fact, he fell ill with severe abdominal pains a week later. He said it was nothing, he'd had these pains before and got over them. But they grew worse. By January 19th, his condition was serious; the doctor held little hope. On the 21st, his mother came as he was given the last Sacraments. She then had to return to look after her other children. About midnight, he turned to Don Bosco at his side and murmured, "This is it, help me, Don Bosco; tell my mother I am sorry for all the trouble I've given her, tell her to have courage; I'll wait for her in heaven . . . and you, and all my friends". He was still only fourteen. (He was suffering from appendicitis; the first operation for that was still forty years away.) A brave little battler, was Michael and his death was a heavy blow to the sensitive Don Bosco, who felt he must tell the world about him. From his brief book, many others have been written, perhaps the best of them in English, "GENERAL MICKEY," by Father Peter Lappin, SDB, a fine present for any boy.

War is a Cruel and Evil Thing

In that year of 1859, the madness of war had again spread to Europe. A Napoleon who had proclaimed himself the Emperor Napoleon III, and in consort with the Piedmontese King, Victor Emmanuel II, rejected an ultimatum from the Austrian Emperor, Franz Joseph. Sixty thousand Piedmontese troops were mobilized while a hundred and twenty thousand French troops assembled to join them. The Austrians, with 160,000 advanced rapidly across the border in an endeavour to defeat the Piedmontese before the French could arrive. They made rapid progress but were held some thirty-five miles from Turin. Meanwhile the French vanguard paraded through the city streets to the wild acclamation of the people. Don Bosco's comment was that there is no glory in war, only cruelty and evil.

By June 24th both sides were drawn up for battle south of Lake Garda, in what we now call the battle of Solferino. The carnage was dreadful and by the end of the long day, fourteen hours of battle, the Austrians were repulsed, leaving, all three armies, more than 30,000 dead and dying on the field. Henri Durant, who was there, described the horror of the aftermath, of the thousands lying maimed and uncared for; he was later to form the International Red Cross.

The upshot of it all was a change of heart by the French Emperor, who made peace with the Austrians, without reference to his Piedmontese allies, and returned with his army to France. Early in the new year of 1860, Garibaldi took his 'Mille,' '1000,' through Italy to capture Sicily and central Italy. In February, the new Parliament proclaimed Victor Emmanuel 'King of Italy,' *all* Italy. He was not master of all the land but the title was enough. The Papal States still retained their precarious independence.

Chapter Thirty

LONG HIKES AND GOOD HARVESTS

SCHOOL HOLIDAYS ARE, or were, long in Italy, well into October, in the early days of which there was the gathering, by all the family, of the "vendemmia," the vintage, the grape harvest, for the wine industry. For many years Don Bosco used to take a group of boys to his home farm at the Becchi where his good-natured brother, Joseph, and his wife, put them all up cheerfully, in return, no doubt, for a spell or two in the vineyards. There would be about twenty to start; later on, this became an important part of the school programme and a veritable expedition of over a hundred boys would set out as soon as the classes ended. In the final stages, which ended in 1864, the party travelled far and wide, in trains, sometimes offered free by the State. But for less ambitious projects, the Becchi would be the headquarters and every day or so the boys would go on foot to villages and shrines all previously worked out by Don Bosco; a couple of donkeys would carry such things as musical instruments, simple stage props, etc., because they would always repay the bounteous hospitality of the villagers with a concert. The band would line up shortly before entering the village and bring everyone to the doors or in the streets, as they marched in to resounding music, cheers and church bells. When long journeys were arranged, the expedition would stay the night, or nights, the village providing beds, sometimes of leaves or straw, in barns, with food and wine in abundance. There would be a special welcome for Don Bosco, some of the good folk kneeling to ask his blessing or kiss his hands; he would give a talk after night prayers and sometimes at Mass.

One of the offshoots of these travels through the villages was the attraction of many splendid vocations. For instance, in the village of Lu Monferrato, the Rinaldi family lined up ten sons, graduated like the pipes of an organ. Number eight was a bright five year old, Philip. On leaving the village, Don Bosco spoke to each boy but to Philip specially, looking at him intently. In due time Philip became a Salesian, and the third successor of Don Bosco as Rector Major. More of this later.

In another village, a boy of twelve heard the drums of the band and raced into the main square, pushing with much elbow power right into the first row of spectators. Don Bosco noticed his interest and asked if he would like to join these boys at school in Turin, to learn to play himself. His parents agreeing, Luigi Lasagna started school with the rest; but he was country born, country fed, and after a couple of weeks, was homesick enough to run away. Then he asked if he might return. Some of the young Salesians were not in favour, but Don Bosco said, "No, bring him back. There's a good stuff in that boy, you'll see!" There was: there was never a better Salesian than Luigi Lasagna, who became the Salesians' second bishop, after Cagliero, and a truly great missionary in South America.

Drought and the Promise of Rain

The Lasagna village was called Montemagno, where they still tell of a remarkable event two years after this visit by the boys. Don Bosco was invited to give a triduum in preparation for the feast of the Assumption. There had been no measureable rain for three years and the vines were dying. As he began his first talk, he said to the large congregation: "If you make this triduum well, make your confessions, and all of you go to Holy Communion, I promise you in the name of Our Lady that the rains will come". When he got back into the sacristy, he found the parish priest in no happy mood.

"I must say you were a bold man to say such a thing!"

"Such a thing as what?"

"Why, to promise it would rain if they made the triduum well, rain on the feast day."

"Did I say that?"

"You certainly did and everybody heard you; and I must say I don't like this sort of thing. If it is a fiasco . . . ?" Certainly many of the more sophisticated thought it would be a fiasco as the day of the feast, August 15th, turned out to be one of the hottest, with implacable blue-bronze skies all day, and right up to the final evening service. Don Bosco himself could only pray fervently as he went into the pulpit; then, after a few minutes, the people started looking at each other, the crowded church began to darken, soon there was the roll of thunder, and lightning, and then a deluge! 'Our Lady's Promise' made that sermon the best ever preached in Montemagno! But no-one was more grateful to Her than Don Bosco himself, grateful *and* vastly relieved!

The final trip of all was in 1864, when the itinerary included the village of Mornese, not far from Genoa, involving a train journey. We shall have more to say about this but for the moment it is enough to say that the good people gave a wonderful welcome to the boys, encouraged by their great parish priest, Don Pestarino. After night prayers, Don Bosco gave a brief talk in the village square; a young woman, Maria Mazzarello, pushed her way to the front, the better to hear and study Don Bosco. Some of the older matrons made disapproving remarks, but Maria said to herself, "They say he is a saint and now I am sure of it". She was to be the co-foundress and first Mother General of the Salesian Sisters, and of such outstanding holiness that she was canonised on June 24th, 1951.

These three, Rinaldi, Lasagna, Maria Mazzarello, were themselves a splendid harvest from the October trips; but there were many others from these and other families, even to our own days.

Don Rua Ordained

We have jumped to 1864; but 1860 had two outstanding events for Don Bosco. The first on June 23rd, was the loss of his greatest friend, his spiritual father and guide, his unfailing supporter, Don Cafasso. News that he was ill came too late for Don Bosco though he raced to the sick room; Don Cafasso had already gone to God. This wonderful priest was yet another Turin saint and was canonised on June 22nd, 1947.

But God made up for the grievous blow to Don Bosco by, a month later, July 1860, giving him the inestimable gift of the priestly ordination of Michael Rua. Don Rua, as he now became, was Don Bosco's 'other half,' his 'alter ego,' and his ordination to the priesthood meant so much to Don Bosco that there was a marked change in him. He was now freer, he could pass on much of the responsibility to Don Rua, could feel able to go out to seek alms and help for his work. The Salesian ideal was safe in Michael Rua's hands.

400 Rolls in an Empty Basket

By 1860, the Oratory had grown to an immense school, with nearly 500 students and 300 working in the trade schools; for most of them Don Bosco had to find almost everything.

Francesco Dalmazzo was fifteen when he came to join one of the higher classes; he came from a comfortable home and did not take kindly to the rather spartan conditions at Valdocco. He revered Don Bosco but found conditions too much and so wrote to ask his mother to come to take him home. However, he decided first to make a last confession to Don Bosco and knelt at his confessional during the morning Mass. He was next in turn when two older boys came to the priest and told him there was no bread for the breakfast. Breakfast consisted of a "pagnotta," a substantial bread roll and water from the tap! Later there was coffee and milk. "Go to the bakers quickly and fetch the bread, then." "We've been and he won't send any more until he is paid and the Bursar says he hasn't any money." "All right, I'll come myself and see to it; gather what rolls there are."

What followed Francesco later recorded in considerable detail. Briefly, he followed Don Bosco to the kitchen, where they gave him a basket containing 'between fifteen and twenty rolls'. The boys lined up outside the door and Don Bosco distributed to them each a roll; many of them kissed his hand and he had a smile and joke for them all. There were about 400 boys and all received their breakfast roll. Francesco says he stood right behind Don Bosco, watching the whole proceeding. When all was over, he looked into the basket as it was taken away and there were still the fifteen to twenty rolls. His mother, standing near, called him rather impatiently to hurry; but he could only go across to her to say he was sorry she had the journey but he could now no longer leave Valdocco after what he had seen. Here was the hand of God, indeed.

Eyes White, Like Two Mushrooms

He became a Salesian priest and was very near Don Bosco, being in later life entrusted with many important posts. He kept a diary and has left us interesting accounts of the many remarkable events he witnessed, including that of the '400 rolls in an empty basket'. He recounts later how he was once in the sacristy with Don Bosco when a woman came in bringing her little niece, begging the priest's blessing. The child was quite blind, indeed, her eyes, attested Don Dalmazzo, had no cornea, 'they were white, like two mushrooms'. Don Bosco asked the aunt and the child if they loved Our Lady; they assured him that they did. After giving them the blessing of Our Lady, he pulled out a medal of the Madonna and showed it to the child, in spite of the aunt's whispered insistence that it was quite useless. The medal slipped from the child's hands and rolled into a dark corner. She ran after it and picked it up, then, realising what had happened, cried out, "I can see, I can see!"

When the question arose of sending the Salesians to England, Don Bosco sent Don Dalmazzo ahead to report on the possibilities. It appears that the fog and the general environment of the proposed foundation appalled him and his advice was hesitant, in spite of which, Don Bosco sent the first three to Battersea, London, in November 1887, his last personal foundation. Don Dalmazzo himself was the official Salesian representative at the Vatican for some years; it was in Rome in 1895, that he met his death at an assassin's hands.

By now, he must have met in Heaven the little blind girl he first saw in Valdocco that 16th of May, 1869. Her name was Maria Stardero. In 1916, she returned to Valdocco to confirm that her sight was still perfect. She was then in her sixtieth year and had had no trouble at all. And she added something that Don Dalmazzo did not know. The old aunt who brought her to Don Bosco was at that time suffering greatly from acute rheumatism in her back and in her right arm. After Don Bosco's blessing, the pain at once disappeared and never came back. A bonus from Our Lady!

We must make room for one more event with rather a different ending.

A woman came to see Don Bosco, bringing her son whose eyes were bandaged.

"He can't stand the light, Father; he screams with pain if I take the bandage off." Don Bosco suggested they say a little prayer together, blessed the boy and then suggested they take the bandage off. The boy smiled as the priest asked, "Can you see all right? Does the light hurt you?"

"Oh, yes, I can see all right but the light doesn't hurt me a bit now!"

The mother frowned, "Now don't say that just because you are here. I am quite sure your eyes must hurt you!"

"No, Mum, they don't now."

Don Bosco suggested he go over to the window and look out at the sunlit grounds. The boy showed his delight as he looked but the mother would have none of it.

"Oh, you're just putting on an act. You'll start your screaming at any moment now!" She seemed so incensed that Don Bosco thought she was going to box the child's ears!

"Why, don't you want your son to be cured?" he asked. The reply was lost as she angrily pushed the boy out of the room, with no thought of thanks in any shape or form. Well, it take's all sorts . . . !

Chapter Thirty-One

THE GREAT SANCTUARY

ALL HIS LIFE Don Bosco attributed the success of his work to the guidance and support of Mary, the Mother of God. She showed him in 'dream-visions' the signposts of his progress, what he would achieve; the *how* she left to him to work out, but actively seconding his work in her own wonderful way.

Adjacent to the original Pinardi property was a large field, growing potatoes, cabbages, lettuce, and the rest. In one of his 'dreams', as far back as 1844, Don Bosco saw himself, with the 'Noble Lady', in this field. She pointed out the first beginnings of his work, the first poor chapel. In later 'dreams', the scene changed and he saw a church, much larger, and other buildings; finally, next to the church, she showed him a magnificent cathedral-like building, which covered, with its other buildings, the whole of the old potato field. Over the entrance to the nave was a white façade in which was written in large capital letters: HIC DOMUS MEA: INDE GLORIA MEA. "Here is my House, whence shall go forth my glory." God's supreme glory.

The word "Valdocco" is an abbreviated corruption of the ancient Latin, "Vallis occisorum" "Valley of the Slain," the 'slain' being two soldiers of the Theban Legion, who became Christians, Aventor and Ottavius. "On this spot," said the Lady, "the two martyrs died" (and she put out her foot to indicate the exact place, which Don Bosco carefully noted) "and it is on this spot, sanctified by their blood, that I want God to be honoured." (A golden cross on the pavement in the crypt now marks the spot.)

It was after a long evening hearing confessions that Don Bosco confessed to being almost haunted by the need to build the 'third' great church of the dream. "Our present church is too small now we have hundreds of boys; this new church will be the Mother Church of our Society."

As ever, the Father Bursar objected: "We haven't enough money even to pay for the stamps we need to send out all the begging letters as it is; how can you talk of more, and gigantic, building!" That had no meaning for Don

Bosco: "When did we ever have any money to do anything? If God wants it, He'll send the means".

Easily said but getting those means took years of weary work for Don Bosco and even more so, Don Rua; they cut down their sleep, they toiled night and day on fund-raising schemes, sweating blood and tears. It certainly demanded faith. The foundations were put in hand at once and when they were ready, the priest turned to the contractor, Carlo Buzzetti, (Giuseppe's brother) to say, "I'd better give you something on account". He pulled out his purse and emptied it into the poor man's hands – forty cents!

"It's all right, Carlo, don't worry, you'll have it all in good time!"

Often the work had to stop for lack of funds; but help would come and they would start again. Don Bosco put the whole project squarely into the hands of his Madonna and how she responded! The word got round of hopeless cases being cured, problems solved against all hope. As people flocked to Don Bosco with their sad stories, he would recommend they first put their souls in order by good confessions and Holy Communion, then start a novena, saying simple prayers for nine days, and he would give them the "Blessing of Our Lady Help of Christians". Offerings flowed in, with startling stories of healing, so much so that Don Bosco began to worry. A Mgr. Bertagno testified under oath at the canonical process for the beatification of Don Bosco, that, at a Retreat, the priest came to him, troubled by the flood of cures, and asked him if he should continue to promote them. "I advised him to continue, for it was plainly God's work."

Our Lady intercedes, God grants, we know, but Don Bosco was afraid that the grateful recipients of all these remarkable graces were attributing them to him, to his prayers, insist though he did that it was Our Lady who was doing it all.

Provocative Title

Of course, he had to ask the permission of the municipality before he could start to build. They seem to have been concerned only with the title, "Mary Help of Christians". "Why that, somewhat provocative, title? Could you not call it the church of Mount Carmel, or of the Rosary? . . . the Madonna has many titles."

"If that's all that's worrying you," laughed Don Bosco, "just give me permission to go ahead and we'll think about the title later on." *We* might see nothing to worry about in the title but in those days of friction between Church and State, there was deep suspicion. Of course, the title "Help of Christians" remained, for, as Don Bosco wrote, "This title, is a compendium of all Church History. When we invoke Mary as the Mother of the Church, she it is who saves Popes, and Bishops and people in difficult times."

Fairy Tale Come True

In September 1866, Don Bosco climbed the high ladders to the cupola, following a delighted boy, the son of generous benefactors; together they laid the final stone. There was still much to do but on June 9th, 1868, the Sanctuary was opened and consecrated, as free of debt. Mgr. Riccardi, Archbishop of Turin, said the first Mass, followed by Don Bosco, whose feelings need no recounting. In addition to what the papers called 'a distinguished congregation,' room was found for 1,200 boys. To them in particular, he poured out his thanks to his Madonna.

"You see, you boys, and especially you older boys who have come back, you used to laugh at Don Bosco's fairy tales about the wonderful things you would see. Well, now, you are in one of them, this marvellous church, a lovely fairy tale church, that Our Lady built herself, because every stone, every piece of marble, came through Her, in one way or another! How we ought to thank Her and ever show Her our trust and our love!" After World War II, the church was further enlarged and beautified and was raised to the rank of a Basilica.

A Reminder

Father Teresio Bosco, author of the best life of Don Bosco in recent years, to which this short account owes a great deal, reminds us that biographers must not give the impression that Don Bosco in these years was the 'only pebble on the beach,' as if Our Lady and all Heaven were concentrating their interest and benevolence only on that rather murky district of Valdocco. Wonderful indeed as their help to Don Bosco was, he was by no means the only builder of great churches to the glory of God; he was not the only priest caring for social misfits, not the only one working in hospitals and prisons, running oratories, running evening classes. During the very times we have been describing, four great parish churches went up in the city of Turin, all the work of dedicated, hardworking, devout priests and people. One church, with its various parochial buildings, actually cost almost 500,000 lire more than Don Bosco's 'Sanctuary'. The Spirit of God is active everywhere, fruitful in creation. Well, we can't tell everybody's tale, but while we concentrate on Don Bosco's, we acknowledge with admiration the work of many other great men and women of God.

Chapter Thirty-Two
NEW PHASES OF THE WORK

THE 'LITTLE FATHER,' Don Borel, once told the boys that cabbages thrive better when they are transplanted; and as the number grew in his infant Society, Don Bosco could never stop transplanting the young shoots. By 1865 there were eighty Salesians, of whom eleven were priests in three Salesian Houses, two of them colleges, and more later. There were losses, too, the biggest and saddest being the death of Don Alasonatti, such a rock of dependence and quiet self-sacrificing work, a grievous blow for Don Bosco. Don Rua, who had been sent to open the new college of Mirabello, was brought back to take his place in the Oratory and at once entrusted with a mountain of work and responsibility. Don Bosco himself found his time more and more taken up with interviews; people would queue on the steps leading to his room, seeking a blessing, a prayer, to give a donation, the sick, the people with problems. His entire mornings used to go, and that meant that more and more, business letters, normal correspondence of all kinds, went into Don Rua's 'in' tray; on the top of all that, was the gigantic labour of funding the 'Sanctuary'. It began to be too much even for his willing spirit.

Don Rua's Collapse

Don Bosco always said that Michael Rua did three men's work; for that, he never slept enough, never ate enough, never rested enough, in fact, never rested at all. And on July 29th, of this year of 1868, he collapsed. The doctor diagnosed peritonitis, too advanced, in his exhausted state, to give much hope. Don Bosco was away and found the Oratory in considerable alarm when he got back. Oddly enough, in spite of urgent pleas to go to see Don Rua at once, he went to hear confessions; and then, still more surprisingly, to have some supper; nor did he seem to be in the least worried. Finally he went up to find poor young Michael seemingly at his last gasp. "Is this the end for me, Don Bosco? Please tell me if I am going to die?" "Die? Of course you're not! I just can't do without you! Even if we threw you through the window, Michael, you wouldn't die! There's far too much to do!"

On the table was the phial for the Holy Oils; in those days of "Extreme

Unction," they were administered really as the *last* anointing, you had to be at death's door. "You can take these away, Father," Don Bosco said to the anxious priest who had brought them up, "they are not needed just yet". Neither were they. In a few days the patient showed signs of marked improvement. In a couple of weeks, Don Bosco sent him away for a month's rest and recuperation and he came back, much improved, to tackle, uncomplainingly, another mountain of work. Some years later, a young Salesian asked Don Bosco if it were true that some Salesians had died of overwork.

"If they did, it would be no disgrace to our Society; but in fact there was only one who was a victim of overwork and that was Don Rua, and you see him today, still doing three men's work."

New Directives for the Salesians

On the political front, the impulse for a united Italy grew even stronger. The Court still favoured an independent Papal State, the Liberal anti-clericals and their adherents, opposed it. Italy as a whole had 22,000,000 inhabitants, of whom 80% could neither read nor write. There was grave unrest still in industry where employers were still paying meagre wages for a twelve hour day. After Karl Marx's 'Manifesto,' unions proliferated throughout Europe, indeed the world, and workers everywhere protested, demanding fair conditions and fair pay. There were said to have been five thousand strikes in Europe alone, many put down by the military, with hundreds of deaths. In Chicago, strike leaders were hanged. Nevertheless, it was to the West that the eyes of the depressed millions were turned. Successive failures of the potato crop in Ireland sent hundreds of thousands to America, the Italians rather preferring the more congenial South America, especially Argentina; 500,000 were said to have emigrated in one year. It was to these, "our compatriots, suffering in ignorance" that Don Bosco was soon to send his Salesians on rescue missions.

In the meantime, the Liberal State was not having all its own way. There was a Catholic reaction and soon all over Italy 'Catholic' associations began to appear: Catholic unions, Catholic banks, Catholic insurance companies, Catholic schools and colleges. Don Bosco joined in this movement to the limit of his resources. He did not, of course, forsake his work for the abandoned poor; every new Salesian House had its 'Festive Oratory,' there were 'hospices' for the trade school boys. But to compete with the State schools it was essential to open more Catholic secondary schools, colleges which usually had boarders, to provide a solid, Catholic educated body of men, fitted to have a voice in the direction of their country. Don Bosco and the Salesians were not of course the only religious society to open these schools. Longer established Orders made, at the beginning, far greater contributions to the demand for Catholic education and it was the work of these dedicated religious men and women, working without salaries, that enabled the poor to take their place in these schools. For the Salesians, Don Bosco followed the advice of Pius IX: they were to continue their work for the poor: in their colleges, they were to charge only minimum fees; they were not to accept schools for the well-to-do.

The new Salesian colleges started with bare boards, the young communities (the first Rectors themselves were all in their twenties!) submitting cheerfully to spartan conditions. Fees were indeed minimal but very often poverty-pleading parents were excused even these. In the early years, before they could organise their own fund-raising schemes, Don Bosco had often to come to the rescue of his hard up youngsters.

Fearful stories are sometimes told how he would send them to take charge of a bare House with little more than their fare in their pockets. It was a hard school, hard training, but they survived. In real trouble he was the kindest and most concerned of fathers. In 1864, a Don Bonetti was the bursar at Mirabello, which was struggling. He had many problems, was feeling miserable from a persistent cough and, truth to say, was very, very sorry for himself. He wrote to Don Bosco. Here is the lovingly preserved reply:

Dear John,

As soon as you get this letter, you are to go straight to Don Rua and tell him he has to cheer you up! You are not to think of saying your Breviary until after Easter. I just forbid you to say it. When you say Mass, take your time about it, don't tire yourself. As for fasting this Lent, I forbid it all. Eat what you need with a good conscience. The good Lord is preparing some new work for you but doesn't want you to even think about it until you are perfectly well again, not having even one little cough left. Make up for it all by saying a few more little prayers, accepting your troubles with patience, giving what good example you can. You will please Our Lord with that.

I was forgetting one thing. See that you have a good mattress on your bed, making yourself comfortable just as you would for some delicate old chap who likes his bed soft! In bed and out of bed, just look after yourself and get well again soon. Amen!

Yours with all affection,
D. John Bosco

This, from one who was known for his personal merciless austerity! You just couldn't raise another grumble after that, could you?

Chapter Thirty-Three

MAN ON A WHITE HORSE; PRELUDE TO THE SISTERS

THE RIDER WAS the Reverend Don Giovanni Bosco, bringing up the rear, following his Valdocco band and boys, plus half the children of the village into the village of Mornese. It was October 1864 and what was to prove the last major October hike; later hikes were nearer home.

They had set off by train, a free trip from the railway, from Turin to Genoa, thence, after a long walk, to Mornese. News of their approach had gone ahead and the children flocked out to meet them. As they came, after sunset, into the main street, there were lights everywhere, fireworks going off, church bells ringing and everybody shouting a welcome. Outside the church was the smiling Don Pestarino who had transformed this sleepy village into a fervent Catholic community. It was he who had sent the white horse to bring Don Bosco in after the long day on foot.

Proceedings were short that first night. Night prayers in the village square after which a few words from Don Bosco thanking them for their welcome and for the hospitality they were offering to him and his boys. Foremost in the crowd was the young woman Mary Mazzarello; she did not want to miss a word. "I am sure he is a saint." It was a day marked in Heaven for from it came great things for God.

Mary was twenty-seven. She and a friend had set up a dressmaker's shop where she put into practice her membership of the Sodality of Mary Immaculate, that was, helping others. Especially the young. They taught the village girls to sew, but also to pray with their work, to sing, to play games in their little courtyard; it was already a little 'festive oratory' after the heart of Don Bosco, a small corner of happiness.

One day a travelling salesman knocked at their door. Two little girls half hid behind him. "My wife has died," he said, "and I cannot look after these children. Could you help me?" Mary looked at their tear-stained faces and swept them up in her arms. It was not long before others came until there were seven such 'orphans'. Other Sodality members wanted to join Mary to help; Don Pestarino, who was all in favour, turned over his own house to them.

Don Bosco's party stayed five days at Mornese and such was the enthusiasm of the people that it was decided to build a school for boys (in those days the poor girls were given scant thought) if Don Bosco would send his Salesians to run it for them, which he gladly promised. The chronicles record the happy ending of the visit. The entire village lined up outside the church after Mass, many offering gifts of eggs, cheeses, choice grapes, chickens, bottles of wine, even a five gallon barrel of the local produce!

As Don Bosco, embarrassed, simply expressed his thanks and began to move away, the crowd cried, "You must bless us before you go!" "I do indeed bless you," he said, "I bless you and your families and your fields with all my heart that God may keep you from all harm, blessing you in all your undertakings; I beg you in turn to pray for me and my boys."

The White House

One day Mary Mazzarello, walking on the fields, looked across the valley to the village of Mornese on the opposite hill and was astonished to see a large white building, where no such building could possibly be; in the attached playground she saw Sisters and girls playing with enthusiasm. She rubbed her eyes, blinked and stared; and then it was no longer there. She said nothing at the time, but wondered.

Ably supported by Don Pestarino, she continued her work amongst the children and more village girls came to join her, though most still lived at home. Since the Sodality of Mary Immaculate was a country wide organisation and was still active in the parish, Don Pestarino thought it better to give Mary's group the name of "Daughters of Mary Help of Christians". The great 'sanctuary' was being built at the time and it is obvious where this title came from. Don Pestarino asked to be admitted to the Salesian Society and was accepted, but Don Bosco asked him to continue his work in Mornese where he was quite indispensable. Meanwhile the project of building the 'boys school' had begun, with voluntary labour.

About this time, Don Bosco conceived the idea, no doubt fostered by Our Lady of doing for girls what he had done for boys. He called his 'Superior Council' together and discussed the matter with them. He gave them time to ponder over it; in the end their opinion was unanimous that a Society of Sisters should be formed. In August 1871, he went to Rome to discuss the matter with the Pope, Pius IX, whom he found very much in favour; "They must do for girls what your Salesians are doing for boys. Draw up draft Constitutions for them; they should depend on you and on your successors". In Mornese was the readymade cradle.

In January 1872, Don Pestarino called the "Daughters of Mary Help of Christians" together and suggested that they begin to live in community. Twenty-seven of them voted to elect a Superior. Twenty-one named Mary Mazzarello. She protested her unsuitability. She had never been to a school, although she could read and write. She was thirty-five and would have to start studying standard Italian since she spoke only the local dialect. Don Bosco, however, confirmed her as Superior, understanding that by her gifts of nature and of grace she was well qualified. He sent her a draft of the proposed 'Constitutions' for her comment.

Black Looks and Healing Death

Meanwhile the 'do-it-yourself' building was going ahead, the villagers working hard and generously. Then came a blow. A new Bishop decided that a school in Mornese could conflict with a junior seminary he was sponsoring not far away and reversed his predecessor's decision. Loyalty to the Bishop sealed the lips of the two priests concerned; Don Bosco took the blame, instructing Don Pestarino to tell the villagers that he could not now undertake to run the school for them. This not unnaturally roused the ire of the poor villagers who had given up so many weekends in hard work. Matters did not improve when the local Council of the Commune decided that Mary Mazzarello's group should occupy the building since in their care for the orphans they were doing public service.

Against the open hostility of their friends and relations in the village, it took all of Mary's unfailing optimism and leadership to hold her little group together, made all the more difficult by their stark poverty. Their farmer mothers and fathers were only partially reconciled to losing their daughters; it seems that every Italian mother looks forward to being the "Nonna," the grandmother, to many children. Mary's own mother may well have been one of these but her splendid father was always her best and staunchest supporter and many a basket of food went quietly to that house, now the 'white house' of Mary's daytime vision.

Nevertheless, there was great joy among all the Sisters when the crucial day dawned, August 5th, 1872, their official birthday. Fifteen Sisters received the habit, eleven made the first, triennial, vows. Don Bosco mentioned their troubles but assured them that they would pass if they had courage and trust in God and Our Lady, their patron, the Help of Christians, whose 'Daughters' they now were, officially.

On January 29th, 1874, the first death came. One of the happiest and youngest, Sister Maria Poggio, fell ill and without fuss, quietly slipped away. Her funeral, attended by her sorrowing young companions, saying the rosary through their tears as they walked, suddenly moved the assembled people and from then on, all hostility ceased, and the true Christian kindness of these simple country folk came through. Don Pestarino had done his work well; and on the very day, shortly after, when he was telling the Sisters that "death could come upon us at any hour, any minute," he fell and died, aged only fifty-seven. Without him there would never have been so firm a foundation for what has become one of the great 'Orders' of the Church.

Every Stitch an Act of Love for God

We have seen something of the mystery of grace in Dominic Savio. Mary, born five years before him, showed from her earliest childhood something of the same extraordinary intuitive cooperation with grace. She knew the value of the Mass and the sacraments. She was conscious of the abiding presence of God, not as an accusing monitor but as a loving Master whom it was a joy and privilege to serve, to do something for. She had heard at Mass the preacher quoting St. Paul, "Whatever you do, whether you eat or drink, do it for the love of God". So she would tell her little girl apprentices, "Every stitch we make, let's do it for the love of God," just to show Him we love Him, "not only when we say our prayers but when we have our dinner, when we sing our hymns or comic songs, when we play games, when we have to stay in to finish some work". This simple creed for the children was also valid for her young Sisters. In her talks to them, in her advice to them, in her practical letters, there was always this theme of joy, of happiness because whatever we did, we did for the love of Our Lord.

Superiors in religious communities have to be careful to observe to perfection both the letter and the spirit of their Rule. Mary, of course, was exemplary in this but she did not forget her humanity. Sister Margaret Renshaw tells us a delightful story of this. It seems that when the first Sisters received their habit, they wore only a head scarf. It was decided that they should have a veil, like all the other Orders. There was considerable excitement when the veils arrived and giggles when the Sisters began to try them on. But, alas, there were no mirrors. By order. But one bright daughter of Eve produced a solution. She filled a bucket to the brim from the well in the courtyard. (It is still there, the well, not the bucket.) She looked into it and put her veil straight. Whereupon the others did the same, and so, laughing like the rest, did Mother Mary Mazzarello. They loved her for it.

The First Swarming of the Bees

After only four years, in 1876, the first 'bees' began to swarm. The first three went off on a freezing February morning to open a school and oratory thirty-five miles away. As more prospective novices came in, twenty-six professed Sisters left Mornese that year, for work, some of it in concert with the Salesians. Seven of them went off to a seaside home for scrofulous children, among the seven being Sister Enricchetta Sorbona, working with cheerful loving care, remembering the day when she herself had knocked at the door of Mornese, holding on to four sisters, each tinier than herself.

In 1875, Don Bosco had sent off his first missionaries to Argentina. For the third expedition, in 1877, he asked Mother Mazzarello for some Sisters. She at once chose six, of many volunteers. They were asked to go to Rome where Pius IX must have been astonished to meet the 'Superior' of the group, aged twenty-two. The second in command was just seventeen. She was the only one with any Spanish. These inexperienced, innocent girls faced a life no-one could could tell them anything about. They set off with all Mother Mazzarello's cheerful confidence that they would do great things for God. Which they most certainly did. There are heroisms beyond pulling people out of burning houses, heroisms that last years.

Only the Superior Could Obey

Mother Mazzarello had never, after contracting typhus as a girl, been really strong and it was noticeable in 1880 that she was frequently ill. It was when saying farewell to another missionary group of her Sisters in January 1881 that she went down with pleurisy and became desperately ill. She made some recovery but only as a passing phase. In the spring, Don Bosco went to see her. The doctors had been shaking their collective heads and doing her little good with their often painful remedies when she asked Don Bosco what he thought of her condition. He said nothing but began to tell her a story.

"One day, Death came to a convent. He knocked at the door and when it was opened, asked the Sister doorkeeper to come with him. She refused, who would look after the door? He went to the kitchen and asked the Sister cook; she refused, too, for who would cook the meals? He asked each one, in vain, and finally came to the Superior. There was no-one else; so she had to go." Mary understood and accepted it.

As May came in, bringing with it all the glory of the flowers, so beloved by Mary, she began to fail; and on the 14th, she went to God. She was only forty-four and had been for just nine years the Mother General, nine wonderful years of constant growth. She had opened twenty-five Houses, convents, schools, oratories, there were 139 Sisters, with fifty novices waiting in the wings. When Don Bosco died, seven years later, there were 390 Sisters with a hundred novices. Today there are, through God's providence, more than 1,500 foundations throughout the world, with some 17,000 Sisters. Mother Mary Mazzarello wrote no books, in her life there were no miracles that we know of, although there were certain unexplained events. She was the most unassuming of God's servants, but He showed, after her death, by granting miraculous cures through her intercession, that she had indeed served Him with heroic sanctity. She was canonised on June 24th, 1951.

Her immediate successor was Mother Catherine Daghero, then aged twenty-five. She had already been Superior for some years in Turin! Just before taking the habit, she was assailed with a fit of the deepest depression and doubts and wanted to withdraw. Mary Mazzarello told her firmly that the moment she was clothed with the habit, all doubts would disappear, which indeed they did. Mother Catherine ruled the Sisters for the next forty-two years, taking them well into the twentieth century and leaving them a worldwide influence for great good.

Chapter Thirty-Four

PARIS FALLS, ROME FALLS AND A TREMOR SHAKES VALDOCCO

THE STORY OF 'Salesian Sisters' might have seemed to us quite the most important event in these years. Alas, there were other things going on which we cannot ignore. The year 1870 saw two historical events which, each in its own way, shook the world. Pope Pius IX called the bishops of the Catholic world to a new Council (the first in the Church since that of Trent, 300 years before), the chief theme of which was to be the infallibility of the Roman Pontiff. Seven hundred bishops, with heads of religious Orders and others, gathered in Rome for the beginning of this Vatican Council on December 8th, 1869. While they were there, the city of Rome fell to Italian troops.

Don Bosco was in Rome at the start of the Council and twice saw Pius IX, who urged him to add another chapter to his "HISTORY OF THE CHURCH," explaining papal infallibility and also to include this in the current printing of the "CATHOLIC READINGS". Before leaving, Don Bosco handed the Pope a statement written in prophetic language concerning events in the immediate future. By April the Council had approved unanimously of a document, "Dei Filiis," giving a clear exposition of Catholic teaching concerning God, Divine revelation and Faith. It also affirmed that, when perfectly understood, there could be no conflict between science and faith since they both came from God. The Council then, on May 15th, began the debate on papal infallibility. After a month a Bishop could write, "We are embarked on a perilous journey in a ship beset by rough waves, on which we are all seasick". The majority were in favour of a definition, with the Pope, but a strong minority argued that such a definition, as a dogma of faith, could only increase the separation between the Catholic Church and other Christian communities.

However, on July 18th, 1870, the Council accepted the text of the declaration, which was read by the secretary, accompanied by one of the most violent thunderstorms ever experienced in Rome. It declared that it was of faith that the Pope was infallible when defining a doctrine concerning faith or morals as being part of the deposit of divine revelation, this in virtue of the Divine promise to Peter. The Council was adjourned for a month; but before it could resume, the gravest events intervened.

France Falls and Troops Storm the Porta Pia Gate

On July 19th Napoleon III declared war on the Prussians. After one setback after another, the French were finally defeated at Sedan and Napoleon made prisoner. In September the populace declared itself a republic and repudiated the harsh peace terms. They set up a "Commune," based on the Revolution at the start of the century, a new Terror. The French army itself crushed the rising with the utmost ruthlessness and 14,000 were said to have died in the fighting.

In Italy, the fall of the French, considered as supporters of the Pope, was welcomed and the government felt free to go forward to the complete unification of the country by attacking the Papal States. Sixty thousand troops began their march. Several advisors counselled the Pope to leave and a British warship was put at his disposal to take him to Malta. However, this time he declined to leave Rome, a decision in line with Don Bosco's own advice.

The Papal troops put up a resistance when the Porta Pia gate was blown open. The Piedmontese army stormed into the city; the Pope then ordered a surrender to avoid bloodshed. Countless streets throughout Italy commemorate the date; September 20th; Via Settembre XX. Losses were minimal but the repercussions were tremendous. Some thought it was the end of the world, others the end of the Catholic Church, a hope expressed in many Liberal, anti-clerical circles. It was certainly the end of 1,500 years of Papal rule in Rome; it was also the end of the Vatican Council which could not be expected to continue in an atmosphere of conflict, where there was no guarantee of safety or tranquillity. The Pope adjourned it sine die.

A Tremor Shakes the Salesian Society

When the news of the fall of Rome reached Don Bosco, he showed no surprise; it was not news to him. A year later, while waiting on the station at Varazze for a train to Turin, he suddenly fell and became unconscious. A heart attack was suspected as he was taken to the Salesian House. His condition deteriorated and he was finally given the last Sacraments. There was the utmost consternation in Turin; Don Rua was able but young; what was the future of the Society to be? Many Salesians offered their own lives for Don Bosco's. When at last there was a turn for the better, he said himself that he thought he was going to die in Varazze.

He had to spend two months convalescing at Varazze and this gave rise to what we can now call a delightful exchange of letters between two dear Salesian sons of his who would gladly have died in his place. We have met, as an orphan from the cholera epidemic, Pietro Enria, who was sent up at once to help nurse the sick man. Left behind in Valdocco was the ever faithful 'giant' Giuseppe Buzzetti who thereupon gave his friend Brother Pietro strict orders to keep him informed, every day if possible, of progress or decline.

The letters have survived. At the start it was a tearful exchange. To Enria's fears and appeals for more and more prayers, Buzzetti could only reply: "I could not finish your letter of the 23rd for grief and for the tears which I could not contain on hearing that our dear Don Bosco, yours and mine, is suffering every day with new pains". They kept it up for all the anxious weeks. At last the improvement came and then the glad day when Enria could send a telegram: "Papa got up today; festa in house; would love to see you". The news "Papa got up today," spread like wildfire in Turin.

As Don Bosco continued to improve, Enria allowed a few days to elapse without writing, which drew a complaint from Buzzetti.

"Dear Pietro,

Are you still alive? If you are, what about your promise to let me have news every day about Don Bosco? Now don't start trying to tease me."

On February 15th, 1872, the great day came of Don Bosco's return to Turin and to Valdocco. He insisted on going first to the great church of Our Lady Help of Christians, which was packed with his Salesians, friends and boys. Buzzetti led them all with a couple of favourite hymns as Don Bosco prayed in silence. When he turned to thank them all for their prayers for his recovery, the whole church joined him in his special thanks to Our Lady. As he left the church, the crowds streamed out after him and around him. Brother Enria remained on his knees in the sanctuary still praying his gratitude to God until Buzzetti took him by the arm and led him outside. There they threw their arms about each other and wept, like the good simple men they were.

Salesian Sister Margaret Renshaw in "CALLED TO JOY," her delightful little life of Saint Mary Mazzarello, gives us another Pietro Enria story. Later that same year of 1872, when the Salesian Sisters were coming into being, Don Bosco and his Council were gravely discussing what habit the Sisters should wear. (Poor Sisters! These men!) A model was produced, sent from Mornese. But of course, there was no-one to try it on. With no doubt a slightly malicious chuckle, Don Bosco sent for Brother Enria. "Ah, Pietro. You are just about the right size! Just slip this habit on, will you?" "What me? Oh Don Bosco!" Beetroot faced, the poor man did. Buzzetti would never let him forget it.

Chapter Thirty-Five
COLLABORATORS AND CO-OPERATORS

CALL THEM WHAT you like for they mean the same thing, although the second title was made official. From the start, Don Bosco found them at his side, few at first but coming from an ever widening circle as his work became known.

Of all the most faithful, none was nearer, and indeed, dearer to him, than the "padre piccolo," the little father, Don Borel. The most ordinary of men, you would miss him in a group of three, a simple priest who used to tell simple country stories in dialect to the boys. "Yet," said Don Bosco of him, "ten good priests could not have done more good than did this little worker for God." Don Borel died on September 9th, 1873, with Don Bosco at his bedside. He was not a Salesian in name, but, one could say, in love. It was found that all his possessions did not amount to enough to pay for his funeral. This Christian duty Don Bosco gladly undertook, remembering how often, how very often, in his own minor financial crises, the little father had just pulled out his worn purse and emptied it into Don Bosco's hands, regardless whether it held gold or silver or bronze; no matter, take it all, whatever there is. Six Salesian Rectors, boys of the Oratory who had long loved Don Borel, proudly shouldered his small coffin to the cemetery, with Salesian clerics and students lining the way.

As well as Don Borel and Don Cafasso, there were other priests who gave Don Bosco a hand in looking after the boys, in one way or another, even those who did not always agree with him. Don Rua's parish priest once warned him, that "Don Bosco isn't quite right in his head, you know". Don Bosco would have agreed that you would have to be a little mad to undertake some of the things he did! 'Crazy' was a word often heard in his own house!

Perhaps it was the natural role of a woman to look after a family that drew them to his family of children in need. His own mother, Margaret, first; then her sister; then Michael Rua's mother, who presided over the kitchen for twenty years; Michael Magone's mother; "Madame" Gastaldi, the future Archbishop's mother, who, when things had progressed into some kind of order, took charge of the linen and used to line up the boys for inspection on Sunday mornings.

Don Bosco had the gift of charming people of all classes to help in need. He never found it easy to beg, in fact, he felt the humiliation of it keenly, his greatest penance; but Our Lady helping, he won the esteem of the rich, the bankers and the aristocracy who parted with large sums. His Italian list of subscribers sometimes reads like a Court Circular, and from outside Italy, from France, and indeed England from such as the Duke of Norfolk, the Countess de Stackpoole and other, helped by frequent articles in the influential Catholic weekly, *The Tablet*. But of course it was the rank and file, the ordinary working men and women who were his greatest helpers and supporters, not only with their money, but with their practical help, in all the Houses and schools, wherever the Salesians began to work.

Great Ideas Blocked

The ancient Orders, such as the Franciscans and the Dominicans have fostered "Third Orders," lay branches of their followers, for centuries. Don Bosco wanted to form his collaborators even more closely to his work. In the draft of his first "Salesian Rule" submitted to Rome, he boldly included an article by which any lay person could, without taking vows, be a Salesian on the same footing as the professed, an *"extern"* Salesian; they would have to live exemplary Catholic lives, take part in the activities of the Church, work for the poor and under-privileged, just as the Salesians were doing.

Rome would not think of it; extern Salesians indeed! You were a religious with vows or you were not. Don Bosco tried again. He put the offending article at the end, in an appendix, as a suggestion. No, certainly not; if you want your 'Constitutions' to be accepted, you must keep to the accepted practice. (The "Secular Institutes" of today had not been thought of in those days.) So, without these revolutionary ideas, the Salesian 'Rule' was ratified by Rome in 1874, an important step for its future existence in the Church.

Two years later, Don Bosco sent to the Pope a draft set of 'constitutions' for a body he called the "Salesian Cooperators"; they were to assist the Salesians in all aspects of their work, they were to work for their own spiritual perfection in working for the good of others, especially the young. They were the third member of the Salesian family, after the Salesians and the Sisters, though they were not called a "Third Order". The Pope approved.

They were not to be just fund-gatherers for the work of the Salesians;

yes, they could and do help that way; but it was their work, their personal labour and their time in working with the Salesians that mattered. Don Bosco stressed this aspect of his concept of the Cooperator in reply to certain of his Salesians who thought only of the financial aspect of their helpers. In 1884, towards the end of his life, Don Bosco defined his exact idea of the Salesian Cooperator. "The direct scope of the Cooperators is not that of helping the Salesians, but of helping the Church, the Bishops, the parish priests, under the general direction of the Salesians."

The Salesian Bulletin

It was imperative that this growing, eventually worldwide, body of Cooperators should be kept informed of the activities of the whole Salesian Family. To this end, Don Bosco founded, in 1877, the monthly *Salesian Bulletin,* the first few numbers of which he wrote himself. It began as a newsletter, chiefly concerned in those days with the newly arrived missionaries, whose long and often fascinating accounts of their travels and experiences were eagerly read and eagerly followed. The first editor was a Don Bonetti who, when asking Don Bosco to whom he should send this Bulletin, received the answer, "To those who ask for it and those who don't". His own presses printed and published it, it was free in that no subscription was asked, though of course, many sent donations. But it was the great bond of unity between the Cooperators and indeed the whole Salesian Family and is so to this day when it is published in many languages throughout the world.

Perhaps we could quote the 'good Pope John' for a remark about it. "My earliest years were protected and nourished by a cherished little picture of Our Lady Help of Christians. Oh, it was a very simple picture, cut out from the *Salesian Bulletin* which our great-uncle Xavier used to receive and read to us with great relish. I put the holy picture over my bed. How many prayers and how many confidences did I pour out before that humble image! And Mary Help of Christians has always helped me."

Chapter Thirty-Six

HARD HEAD MEETS ITS MATCH

VOCATION IS ANOTHER mystery of grace. The young man in the Gospel upon whom Jesus looked and loved and invited to follow him, turned away. He was free to do so. Yet Our Lord said to the apostles, "It was I who chose you, you did not choose me". God gives a call, gives us grace to accept that call, but we are still free to reject it. Don Bosco who is said to have been concerned in the vocation of 2,000 priests, the majority of them diocesan priests, would never try to force a decision. Except, perhaps, once.

The reader may remember that, when, on his October hikes. he went to a town, or village, called Lu Monferrato, he met a family named Rinaldi whose five year old son, Philip, he looked at with particular care.

The Salesians opened a school not far from Lu and when Philip was ten his father took him there. The young Salesian immediately in charge of him was a kind and gentle Paul Albera, with whom he soon made friends. Another teacher was not either so gentle or kind and when, at the end of a tiring day for both teacher and pupils, he snapped at Philip, that young man kept his temper but marched straight up to the Rector and straight home.

Nothing could bring him back: not even Don Bosco. Not even letters from Don Bosco over the years. When Philip was eighteen, Don Bosco made yet another attempt to bring him back. They were in the sacristy together when a poor woman came in, on crutches and nursing an injured arm. She begged Don Bosco's help. He gave her the blessing of Our Lady Help of Christians and there and then, in front of Philip, she cried out in joy, picked up her crutches which had fallen from her and went out, fully healed. Not even that moved Philip. Not only did he refuse Don Bosco's repeated invitation but began to turn away from his religion, his prayers, getting careless in many things and troubling his parents, who did not cease to pray for him. When he was twenty, a suitable marriage was being arranged; but when the interested parties arrived to discuss it, Don Bosco also arrived and at once tackled Philip. They were good friends but Philip was a hard headed countryman and stood his ground, point after point. Don Bosco was also a hardheaded countryman and he fought his end, point by point. At last

Philip gave in: the parents of the girl departed.

The following November, 1877, Philip went to a house Don Bosco had opened for late vocations and there the twenty-one year old had to settle down to Italian literature and Latin verbs. It was hard going; but the kind Don Albera was now his Rector and that helped. In August 1880 he knelt at Don Bosco's feet and took the three vows. Now a Salesian at twenty-four, he went on at once to theology, although without any great signs of enthusiasm. When the time came for him to take minor orders, he did so only because Don Bosco said he should; the same for subdiaconate and diaconate. On Christmas Eve, 1882, he was ordained priest.

"Now," said Don Bosco, "are you happy?"

The reply startled him. "As long as I am here with you, yes. But if I have to go away, I don't know what I shall do."

However, he did volunteer after a while to go on the missions.

"No," said Don Bosco, "there is work for you to do here."

When Don Bosco died, Don Rua was elected in his stead. When he died, Don Albera, and when he died, Philip Rinaldi was elected Rector Major, in 1922. Such was his reputation (his Cause for Beatification has been introduced) that Don Francesia, who knew Don Bosco for forty years, declared, "Except for the voice, he was Don Bosco himself".

There is no doubt that Don Bosco persisted in his pursuit of Philip Rinaldi because in one or other of his 'dreams' he must have seen him leading his Salesians.

Missionary to Lepers

Stories about vocations abound. One day a country labourer, Michael Unia, aged then twenty-seven, came to Don Bosco to discuss a possible vocation. He wanted to become a priest, but not a Salesian (possibly put off at the thought of teaching!). Don Bosco smiled at him and then said, unusually, "What if I tell you something important, something that might show you God wants you for some special work?"

"You would have to prove that."

"If I tell you something of yourself that only you know, would that be a sufficient sign that God wants you to become a Salesian?"

"All right; tell me what's on my conscience." Don Bosco did.

"How can you possibly know these things?"

"Let me tell you something else. When you were eleven, you were in the choir. One day at Vespers, the boy next to you fell asleep, with his mouth wide open. You had in your pocket some plums and you took the biggest of them and plopped it right into the poor lad's mouth. He woke up, choking, and ran about like a mad man, with you bursting your sides laughing. The Vespers had to stop until order was restored, but the curate gave you half a dozen wallops to remember."

After that, Michael could make no further protests and duly became a Salesian. He found his 'special work' in South America, in Columbia when he volunteered to work as a missionary, the first in the then notorious leper colony of Agua de Dios. There were 730 stricken men and women in that neglected field of human suffering, suffering allied with degradation. Like another Father Damien, Father Unia brought them, little by little, a sense of human dignity and decency, the love of Christ and His healing care. He stayed with them until he died, and his name is revered. He has Salesian successors who continue his work.

Chapter Thirty-Seven

DREAMS OF FAR OFF LANDS

THERE CAN BE no doubt now in any reader's mind that Don Bosco was granted the sight of much of his future work and its development in 'dreams'. Before his death, he agreed with his biographer that these dreams were really 'visions'. There are dreams and dreams. The usual variety may come from possibly, indigestion, of which no doubt Don Bosco had his fair share. Others, rare events, may give the dreamer some vision of past or future events; some of Don Bosco's dreams showed actual events, others were allegorical, portraying evils in the shape of savage beasts. Some of his 'dreams' were not really dreams at all, such as when he saw the "anxious natives hovering over the sick Cagliero's bed"; that was a daytime vision.

Pope Pius IX ordered him to record his dreams and some 160 are in print; some took hours and are in great detail so that they need ten or more pages. It was in familiar conversation with the Pope that Don Bosco first told the following dream and only afterwards to the Salesian biographers. He found himself in a wide plain in a tropical land. The inhabitants were tall, strong, dark-skinned men and women, clad in animal skins, the men with spears and other weapons. He saw approaching these people a group of white missionaries, none of whom he knew; he was horrified to see the 'savages' attack them, cutting them to pieces, exulting as they paraded with heads and limbs on their spears. After a while, he saw another group, and this time recognised the leaders as among his own sons. To his astonishment and relief, the natives welcomed them with smiles, listened to their teaching of Christian truths and began to take part in the services.

For years Don Bosco tried to identify these people, sifting through libraries and journals from all parts. Now one of the side-issues of the Vatican Council of 1870 was the arrival in Italy of Bishops from all over the world, with those from missionary countries taking the opportunity to invite recruits. Don Bosco finally learnt that the natives of his dream came from Argentina, more precisely from Patagonia. In 1874, the Argentine Consul, Señor Gazzolo, brought Don Bosco a request from the Archbishop of Buenos Aires, asking him to send help to take care of the 30,000 Italian immigrants in that city for the most part living in penury and ignorance. He also wanted him to take over a school in San Nicholas, a flourishing centre.

After hearing the affirmative opinion of his Council, Don Bosco agreed to send a group of Salesians in 1875. The Archbishop had made no reference to the evangelisation of the tribal areas, with which Don Bosco was primarily concerned as were the Salesians when he revealed his plans to them; everyone wanted to go. He wrote to the Archbishop, agreeing to send a group in 1875, with these three points: the first would establish a centre in Buenos Aires a base from which to build schools, oratories, etc.; the second would take up the work in San Nicholas, and the third would, from these two bases, prepare to extend the work to other parts. By the latter Don Bosco meant "to extend the work to the tribal lands".

The Missionaries Sail

With characteristic generosity, he made a suggestion to Don Cagliero, his best man, the one the work in Turin could least spare; at thirty-seven, he was already a remarkable personality, preacher, organiser of many projects, master musician, popular and sought after all over the city.

"Giovanni," said Don Bosco, "I need someone to go with the group who can meet the Archbishop, establish contact with the authorities and put the work on a firm footing." "Well, I could go if you want," answered Cagliero. "All right, but for three months; then you come back." The three months lasted thirty years.

With Don Cagliero was to be Don Fagnano, who became a truly great missionary; there were to be six priests in all and four Brothers.

Don Bosco sent eleven missionary 'expeditions' to South America but the first was the most dramatic. It aroused tremendous enthusiasm and excitement and he made the most of it. In preparation they had been studying Spanish and had been to Rome to receive the blessing of the Pope. On November 11th, 1875, the farewell ceremony took place in Turin. The vast church was full to overflowing, festive lights and music abounding. After his emotional talk, Don Bosco received each missionary from the sanctuary and invested him with a crucifix; all the other Salesians then exchanged a farewell embrace. Family, friends and relatives followed suit.

On November 14th, the group embarked from Genoa on the French liner Savoie. The future was not going to be easy. But Don Cagliero carried with him a brief personal note: "Do what you can; God will do what you cannot. Entrust everything to Our Lord in the Blessed Sacrament and to Mary, Help of Christians, and you will see what miracles are." Yes, miracles, but also martyrs. Salesian missionaries have carried the Gospel far and wide but the wine in their Mass chalices has many times turned to blood. They have suffered cruel deaths in many lands. It is true that the "blood of the martyrs is the seed of the Church"; every year that costly seed is still being sown by Don Bosco's sons. May the harvests that follow be rich indeed.

Chapter Thirty-Eight
PATAGONIA, LAND OF PROMISE

THE GOOD SHIP *Savoie* weighed anchor in Buenos Aires on December 14th, 1875. The Salesians found themselves at once among friends, welcomed by the Archbishop and clergy, as well as by some 200 Italian residents, including, wonder of wonders, a group of excited young men who had been boys at the Oratory of Valdocco. It was very wonderful indeed until some stark realities began to manifest themselves. There were 30,000 Italians in the city, 300,000 spread throughout Argentina. Apart from a few, most of them were living in poverty, scratching a living, illiterate, lacking in Spanish and totally abandoned spiritually. Parents who would call themselves Catholics had not even taught their children the words of the sign of the cross, let alone the Hail Mary. News of the arrival of the Salesians brought a flood of requests for schools. A pathetic letter from the neighbouring country of Uruguay, from the Apostolic Delegate, revealed that there was not in that whole country one seminary, nor even one seminary student, and in the capital, Montevideo, not a single Catholic school. Yet Uruguay was listed as a Catholic country!

As arranged, Don Fagnano took six priests with him to open the school at San Nicholas, while Don Cagliero began work in the capital. The "La Boca" quarter was inhabited largely by Italians, dominated by masonic lodges. No priest had ever set foot in that gloomy area, which, of course, made it a first choice for Don John Cagliero. He found himself surrounded by excited children with whom he laughed and joked as Don Bosco had done with the urchins of Valdocco. "Here you are! A lovely medal for the best one here! All right, all right, here you are, you can all have one! I'll be back next week when you have all learnt to make the sign of the cross properly, words and all . . . . Come on, say them after me now!"

The Archbishop soon got to hear of it and sent for Don Cagliero.

"You did a very foolish thing, going there. I've never been in that quarter myself and would not allow any of my priests to go either; it is far too dangerous."

But, of course, Don Cagliero was there again within days with more medals and pictures and making plans for the first 'Oratory'.

But back in Turin, they were all eager to know when the missionaries were going to meet the 'savages'. The Salesians soon found out, however, that the only 'Indians' within a couple of hundred miles were miserable slaves, men, women and children, captured in military sweeps, if anything lucky to be alive for all natives bearing weapons were given short thrift. There was, they discovered, a state of perpetual war between the chiefs and government troops, massacres on both sides, with the natives hating and fearing the better armed troops and whites merciless in their reprisals. Evangelization seemed a remote dream.

The following year, in response to Cagliero's pleas, Don Bosco, sent a larger expedition, of twenty-three, sometimes called the 'children's crusade,' from the extreme youth of six beardless clerics. The following year again, 1877, there were eighteen Salesians and for the first time, six valiant Salesian Sisters, the first of many Daughters of Mary Help of Christians who have since crossed the ocean to South America.

The Archbishop of Buenos Aires, realising that both Don Bosco and Mother Mazzarello had both gone 'beyond the limit of possibility' in sparing these precious people, made an effort to please Don Bosco by trying to arrange for a couple of Salesians to go to Patagonia. Their ship ran into a hurricane and they barely escaped shipwreck; they had to return. However, in 1879, the Minister of War, himself a general, decided to lead an expedition, of 8,000 troops 'to clean up the rebellious tribes'. As a man of some principle, he asked the Salesians to spare him a couple of priests to act as chaplains: the Archbishop added his Vicar General to the party. Each priest was given a personal horse and they shared a wagon carrying their bags, plus an altar, a harmonium and vestments.

Journey into the Interior

The two Salesians, Don Costamagno, and Don Botta, have left vivid accounts of this first journey into the hinterland, accounts which were eagerly read in Turin and at once passed on to the *Salesian Bulletin* throughout Italy. It was a military foray of course, and the cross had to follow the sword; but at least, some contacts were made. The first Indians they met were semi-civilised Pampas Indians, living in huts of animal skins. Some spoke a little Spanish and the priests at once began to speak of God and teach simple prayers.

It was hard going for city bred men; they rode 1,300 kilometres on horseback, through wild, often roadless country; one whole month through a desert. But on the feast of Mary Help of Christians, May 24th, Don Costamagno, riding ahead, crossed the great river Rio Negro into the long promised land of Patagonia.

This was 'conquered country' in general and the missionaries met many Indians living in wretched conditions, some in camps preparatory to going into slavery on white farms; the more fortunate ones who had not taken part in any fighting, were being resettled in cleared areas. Eventually, the missionaries reached the town of Patagones, then with 4,000 inhabitants, and after a short stay there, they returned to the capital, to send their exciting news back home. The military expedition continued for another two years, eventually forcing the warring chiefs, led by Chief Manuel Namancura, deeper into remote mountain valleys.

The upshot of the expedition was that the Archbishop wrote to Don Bosco offering him the vast mission territory based on Patagones, which he accepted amidst general rejoicing. At last, we are a real missionary Society! Two groups took over control, under Don Fagnano and Don Milanesio, two great missionaries, who have left legends behind them. Don Fagnano tried to bring as many Indians as possible to his base at Patagones, while Don Milanesio, a picturesque character with a patriarchal beard and a gift of tongues, roamed the forests seeking out often hidden Indian settlements, quickly mastering their languages and as quickly winning their confidence. One tactic complemented the other and brought considerable success.

When at last Manuel Namancura, the last of the great chiefs, decided to treat with the government, it was to Don Milanesio he turned to act as his mediator, a choice accepted by the government negotiators. Under his protection, the chief laid down his arms at Fort Roca on May 15th, 1883, in exchange for which he was given the rank and uniform of a colonel, with accompanying salary. It was really a triumph for the missionaries. However, although organised resistance ceased, there still remained isolated groups, hidden deep in the vast forests.

I Saw into the Hearts of the Mountains

In that same year of 1883, thousands of miles away, Don Bosco saw in a remarkable 'dream' the future of South America and some of its missionaries. He found himself in a train starting from Cartagena, Columbia, in the north, with as guide, a boy, Luigi Colle, who had recently died. As the train raced 'at a dizzy speed,' to the south, Don Bosco – who had never been out of Europe – was able to give an accurate description of the territory they traversed. He ascribed all this knowledge to his young guide who "explained matters of geology, mineralogy, of flora and fauna". There were areas in which would be found "riches of imcomparable value". When at last the train entered Patagonia, Don Bosco asked if he could visit his Salesians whom he had recently sent out. They stopped outside a town and made their way to the Salesian centre. The size and development of the buildings astonished him but not less astonishing was that when he met the Salesians he did not know any of them. Nor they him.

"But, but, don't you know me? I'm Don Bosco!"

"Oh yes, we have his picture on the wall."

"But what about Don Cagliero, Don Fagnano, Don Costamagno? What about them?"

"Oh, we've heard about them, but they died some time ago."

(Cardinal Cagliero actually died in 1926.)

This was obviously a dream of the future. Nevertheless, when they resumed their train journey, they still witnessed a horrifying cannibalistic killing in a forest clearance; on the banks of a great river, they saw fearful animals, unknown to Don Bosco, which, said Luigi, signified moral evils the Salesians would have to fight against. As they turned north for the return journey, the young guide pointed out enormous deposits of coal, lead, iron, gold, and 'other things more precious than gold'. Don Bosco said, "I saw into the hearts of the mountains". Back at Cartagena, Luigi was showing the priest a wonderful map of their journey, with the future developments, when Don Bosco woke up. He later dictated the six hour 'dream' to a secretary in precise detail. When it was published in South America, it caused a sensation. Geologists and mineralogists worked out the journey and proved the accuracy of the descriptions. The railway, only partially built in 1883, was finally completed and enormous development has followed.

Father Peter Lappin, in his fine book of Don Bosco *Give Me Souls,* adds an interesting modern sequel. Brasilia, the ultra modern capital of Brasil, was founded only in 1960. Don Bosco's dream described a "city beside a great lake," between latitudes 15° and 20°. Brasilia stands exactly between these latitudes. The lake, which did not exist in 1883, was artificially created. The city, Father Lappin tells us, needed a seaport; so one was built at Marau Bay, called Vascopolis, able to take the largest oceangoing vessels. Between Brasilia and Vascopolis runs a super-highway, 1,000 kilometres, 600 miles. Its name? Dom Bosco Way, "Via Dom Bosco," ("Dom" being Portuguese for the Italian "Don").

Don Bosco's last missionary dream came to him in April 1886, when he was greatly enfeebled and could recite it only with difficulty. Again it was a dream of the future. He was shown the development of Salesian missionary activity throughout the world, across which he travelled by means which are not clear; perhaps, in our hindsight, by plane. From South America he passed through the Cape of Good Hope, through central Africa, in which continent there were ten Salesian centres, continuing right across the world to Hong Kong and then to Peking. In this Chinese city, "Salesians from East and West would meet on a bridge". All these events have already been realised; Salesians now work in eighty-five countries.

Chapter Thirty-Nine
SAINTS MUST SUFFER

IN THE ACTS of the Apostles we read how two great apostles and missionaries, Paul and Barnabas, teamed up and did great things for God until, disagreeing over the temporary defection of young Mark, they parted company. They were still great saints, great men; but still men. Men with all man's capacity for misjudgement, for seeing things only from one's own point of view.

At a time when the development of Don Bosco's work seemed at its greatest, he was suffering from the cruellest trials of his life. They came chiefly from his Archbishop, Archbishop Gastaldi, who had been a lifelong friend, born in the same year, their mothers great friends, though Margaret was a farmer's wife and Madam Gastaldi, the Marchioness Fassati, who worked untiringly in the Valdocco Oratory.

One does not want to dwell on unhappy matters, especially now that they are water under the bridge; but something must be said.

Briefly, it began with Mgr. Gastaldi's predecessor, Mgr. Riccardi, who, appointed Archbishop after a long delay owing to political trouble, was anxious to re-establish the Church and needed every help. He was an enthusiastic admirer of Don Bosco's work until one day, it was mentioned that the Constitutions of the new Society had been given a provisional approval in Rome.

"Rome? But I thought you were going to work only in and for this diocese, at the disposal of the Archbishop?" With hindsight, we can see that that restricted scope was not in God's design for the Salesian Society, but the Archbishop did not have that benefit. He saw only one of his diocesan priests ambitiously working for independence, going his own way, without further reference to episcopal authority. The Archbishop from then on showed his coldness and began to impose restrictions on Don Bosco.

When he died in 1870, Don Bosco, who was then on the closest terms with Pius IX, at once suggested that his good friend, Mgr. Gastaldi, then Bishop of Saluzzo, should be given the Archbishopric of Turin. The Pope, who knew the Bishop of Saluzzo better than Don Bosco, hesitated; but, we are told, Don Bosco so pressed his point that at last the Pope gave in. "You want him and you can have him." This was Don Bosco's first mistake, for God was allowing him to be, at least partly, the author of his own misfortune and sufferings. A second mistake was far worse. So pleased was he that he at once sent an advance telegram to Mgr. Gastaldi announcing the appointment before it was published. When later, the new Archbishop began, like his predecessor, to look less approvingly on Don Bosco's training of his young men, Don Bosco sensing the coldness, wrote him a letter, in which he reminded him of their past friendship, adding the fateful words . . "When Mgr. Gastaldi was made Bishop of Saluzzo, it was due to Don Bosco's recommendation, when he was made Archbishop of Turin, it was likewise due to Don Bosco's intervention". It was meant to show with what affection and esteem Don Bosco held him; instead, it aroused the fury of the Archbishop who descended on Valdocco and gave a fiery sermon about his appointment, "an appointment due entirely to the work of the Holy Spirit and to no-one else's intervention," which he repeated several times. For ten years, he showed his resentment.

In his work for the Church, Mgr. Gastaldi was a splendid Archbishop, a gifted organiser, with a wide vision; his love for the Madonna was, in its own way, as deep as Don Bosco's, as was his care for the young. But he would be master in his own diocese and would brook no opposition to his views. He was extremely concerned about his authority and Don Bosco was by no means the only one who suffered in consequence.

In Rome he did all he could to prevent the Constitutions of the Salesian Society from being accepted and increased the restrictions by all the authority given him in law.

So far did he go that for a fancied infringement he once imposed on Don Bosco personally the severest punishment any priest can suffer, that of being deprived of faculties to offer Mass, to preach or to hear confessions. "The sort of thing," stormed one angry Bishop, "we only give to hopeless alcoholics."

Don Bosco had many friends in Rome, but so had the Archbishop and even Pius IX seemed to be affected. When he was dying in 1878, Don Bosco went to Rome, but try as he would to see the Pope, all doors were locked against him. It has since transpired that this was quite contrary to the Pope's wishes.

The new Pope was the great Leo XIII. He knew a great deal about the disagreement but moved quietly at first. At length a friend of Don Bosco's, Cardinal Alimonda, suggested to the Pope a way to prove Don Bosco's virtue. "Ask him to undertake the building of the Sacred Heart church!" This project has been under way for some time, had got bogged down by poor contractors, and had finally ceased, to the distress of the new Pope. In 1880, he called Don Bosco to Rome and explained the trouble. "Would you undertake this building, Don Bosco? I can offer you no money." "The wishes of the Pope are a command to me," said Don Bosco, "I accept." He was building two other churches at the time and as ever hard pressed for money. The building of the Sacred Heart in Rome, humanly speaking, killed him, but Leo XIII had his proof.

The matter of the Archbishop and Don Bosco was discussed in the Vatican in 1881, by eight Cardinals. Two were for the Archbishop, two abstained, four were for Don Bosco. The Pope stopped all further discussion. "Authority must be supported," he said, "but Don Bosco will agree, I am sure."

His solution was hard indeed on Don Bosco, that he should send a letter of apology to the Archbishop, begging his pardon.

The Salesians were furious at the manifest injustice but Don Cagliero stopped all argument, "The Pope has spoken; that's enough". Don Bosco, drinking his bitter chalice, wrote his letter, to which came a reply, "The pardon you have asked for is granted with all my heart".

After the Archbishop's death, the new one, Cardinal Alimonda, was truly a friend of Don Bosco and healed many wounds. The Pope, too, could not have been more anxious to show his esteem and admiration for all the work of the Salesians, at home and abroad. As a sign of this, he appointed Don Cagliero the first Salesian Bishop, a sign to the world of his approval; Don Fagnano was soon to follow as a second Bishop. But it was the building of the Sacred Heart church in the heart of Rome that sealed his esteem for Don Bosco. It was indeed a mammoth task.

Chapter Forty
THE GREAT JOURNEYS

DON GIOVANNI BOSCO was not by nature a man who easily turned the other cheek; readers of his early life would realise that; his reactions as a boy and as a young man were often swift and even violent. Hence the great strain, in later years, of curbing his natural tendencies, the constant efforts of preserving charity and patience, had a visible effect on him which was all too evident in the closing years of the Archbishop Gastaldi regime. Some of his biographers do not hesitate to say that he had been "through hell" and was physically and mentally a "broken man". Be that as it may, while the grace of God was sufficient for him in his sufferings, nevertheless, the appointment as Archbishop of Turin of Cardinal Alimonda was an enormous relief, the greatest grace perhaps he could have had. The Pope, Leo XIII, mentioned the fact to Don Bosco, "In appointing the Cardinal, I thought of you".

The change was immediately evident. The Cardinal himself came to Turin very quietly and discreetly, with no fanfare of trumpets. The times were difficult, political feelings running high, in the long aftermath of the taking of Rome and the excommunications that followed.

After a short delay, Don Bosco wrote to the Cardinal, requesting a meeting and asking when it would be convenient for him to call. The reaction of the new Archbishop to this request was typical. He at once called for his carriage and went posthaste to Valdocco, "It's quicker this way," he smiled, and at once showed his pleasure at meeting Don Bosco. They talked for some time and then went out into the verandah overlooking the playground. As they appeared, at once the band, gathered before the windows, began to play and the boys to applaud. "I wanted to give you a surprise," laughed the Cardinal, "but you have given one to me!" There is no doubt that in the remaining four years of Don Bosco's life, the friendship and kindness of the new Archbishop was a great comfort to the ailing priest at Valdocco.

The Cross of the Sacro Cuore

However, if the saints 'come down from one cross, they are nailed to another'. The burden of the "Sacro Cuore," the great church of the Sacred Heart which Don Bosco had accepted on behalf of the Salesians at the request of the Pope, was indeed a heavy one. He marshalled all his forces, all his experience in gathering funds, he himself working unceasingly, begging from old friends and knocking at new doors at which he was not always well received, but enduring the humiliations as a penance to earn help elsewhere. Don Rua and other Salesians worked overtime in searching for new sources of charity. Money poured in but it was never enough. Building in Rome and for the Pope has a character all its own. Over hundreds of years, the Romans have had a saying that "in working for the Pope, there is always something to eat for everyone". Fair game for workers and contractors. Slow work, shoddy work, exorbitant prices and charges, constant drain of thefts of tools, machines and material; it needed much sharper control than could be exercised by a couple of inexperienced priests who were not Romans.

The Pope had had to stop building and it looked as if Don Bosco would have to do the same. Someone remarked he was looking a little bent; "No wonder," he said, "I'm carrying the weight of the Sacro Cuore!" He could laugh, ruefully, "They say the Church is being persecuted; well, all I know is that it is the church that is persecuting me just now!"

It was then that he came to a decision. He would go outside Italy, he would go to France. "France has always been generous, they have always helped me." Mixed reactions from his friends followed the announcement. Certain 'experts' said it would be a fiasco. "France is just getting over its war with Prussia, it had to pay heavy costs and, as for Paris, Paris is trying to build its own church in honour of the Sacred Heart, the Sacre Coeur on Montmartre, which is costing millions and is nowhere near finished. No, they won't give you a sou!"

Well, he had met faint hearts before. He was old at sixty-eight, so infirm that he needed a strong arm to help him walk: but his heart was high. He left Turin on January 31st and was away four months. He came to Paris by way of Nice, Marseilles, Avignon and Lyons. France knew he was coming and knew all about him. The moment he put his foot on French soil, all doubts vanished. He had made it quite clear what he was coming for and France opened its great heart and its purse. His slow journey was a triumphal progress. No-one could possibly have foreseen the warmth and enthusiasm with which vast crowds greeted "this poor old country curé," as he called himself. At Avignon the streets were decorated; they snipped bits of his cassock, even tried to get locks of his hair! "All the lunatics aren't locked up!" he shook his head. At Lyons they had to put up barricades to control the crowd. One coachman, trying to get through the crush, cursed, "I'd sooner drive the devil than a saint if it's going to be like this all the time!"

It was all breathtaking, beyond all expectations. But now for Paris. What would Paris do? Paris, elegant, sophisticated, inclined to be amused at 'country curés'. How would Paris respond to this simple Italian priest with his hesitant, sometimes almost inaudible French? Political relations between Paris and Rome were distinctly cool at the moment. He need not have worried. He simply smiled at them, loved them and they loved him in return. The papers said, "Paris threw herself at his feet!" They could talk of nothing else. The press columns are there for all to see to this day. They spoke of his appearance, of the crowds, they wrote of miracles, yes, miracles witnessed by many, at once attributed by him to the intercession of the Blessed Virgin. In the manner of journalists everywhere they invented miracles if they did not witness any. Don Bosco insisted, "I am a sinner like everyone else; if you want miracles, you must turn to Mary, she is your mother, she will do wonders if you ask her with humility and fidelity". In the church of the "Archconfraternity for the conversion of sinners" where he was preparing to say Mass, the crowds overflowed outside. "Whatever is going on?" asked a casual visitor. A simple woman answered her, "It's a Mass for the conversion of sinners and it's being said by a saint".

The hierarchy of Paris were warm in their support. In the church of St. Peter, Cardinal Lavigerie introduced him to the congregation, exhorting them to be generous to this priest who was "the St. Vincent de Paul of Italy". The response of all Paris was overwhelming. Half a dozen 'secretaries' worked long hours answering letters and recording the donations. So much came in that once there was simply nowhere to put the money as it poured in, in notes, coins, even jewellery. Don Bosco's day began as early as 5 a.m.; within an hour the crowds waiting to see him were building up; they lined the stairs and the corridors. They wanted to ask him for help, advice, cures, some simply wanted to touch him, even to see him, close at hand. He made himself available for photographs, alone or flanked by Don Rua and Don Barruel, his two companions. Some anti-clerical papers commented sourly on the photographs. Vanity? No, just a means to get his work known. They were useful to a Doctor D'Espiney, who was writing the first French biography; it sold 50,000 copies in a couple of months.

When at last he left Paris by way of Amiens and Lille, he met the same excited jostling crowds . . . and those scissors! "They're just as crazy here as they are in Paris!" But there were tears of gratitude when he spoke of France and its overwhelming generosity. The yield was enormous; but the bottomless well of the Sacro Cuore swallowed it all up. His health was worse but, in 1886, he said, "I must run to France again," which he did against all advice. The doctors said it would be a miracle if he returned; so he made his will. He did return though even further enfeebled. This was a much shorter visit but the enthusiasm was the same. The noble family of Colle themselves gave him the vast sum of 150,000 lire.

Still the church was not finished and not paid for. So, later in 1886, he set off for Spain, being received there with the same generosity. He was able to meet in person the "Mother of the Salesians," Madame Chopitea, the once rich lady who gave her entire fortune away for the poor, much of it to the Salesians for their work. (Her Cause for Beatification has been introduced.) Other Spanish friends gave generously; he was given a site on the hill in Barcelona called "Tibidabo" (Latin from "I shall give you") upon which the Salesians later erected another great church in honour of the Sacred Heart, surmounted by a gigantic statue, which the Communists used for target practice during the 1936 revolution. However, it has survived.

The Final Journey

A year later, he made his last visit to Rome. The journey from Turin took ten days, so feeble was he. But he was determined to be present at the opening, after seven years of unrelenting labour, of the 'Basilica' of the Sacred Heart. It too, is surmounted by a great golden statue of the Sacred Heart, across the street from the central Termini station.

There he said his last Mass in Rome, his first and only Mass in the new church. He had to be supported by two priests, overcome by emotion, with frequent stops. As he was led from the high altar, he looked across at the statue of Our Lady and gasped out, "When I was a boy, She said to me, 'One day you will understand'. Today, I have understood".

"Make yourself humble and strong," She had told him. She had shown him the way in mysterious 'dreams', she had intervened in moments of crisis with power from Heaven, for which he gave her his heartfelt, unstinted praise.

But he and his immediate helpers had earned that help by their own almost terrifying labours in finding the means, year after year, to build churches for the people, schools, workshops and orphanages for the children in need. He had made himself humble and strong but now he was a wreck of a man, exhausted in every function of his body. He had promised total commitment and had kept his promise, with every breath of that body, with every beat of a great heart.

Chapter Forty-One

THE BOY THE BRONZE GIANTS WERE ANXIOUS ABOUT

ALTHOUGH WE SAID that the three months Don Bosco sent Don Cagliero out to Argentina for extended to thirty years, he did return after a couple of years to take over for a while the care of the Sisters and the start of the work in Spain. There is no doubt that of all the boys who came to Don Bosco in the early years, two were nearest his heart; Michael Rua and Giovanni, John, Cagliero. It was natural that as Don Bosco's age and infirmities grew, he should turn his thoughts to his possible successor. He was travelling with Don Cagliero one day when he suddenly asked him: "If I were to die, who do you think could take over the Society?"

"Don't talk about dying yet, Don Bosco."

"No, but let us admit the possibility. I have two, possibly three, in mind. What about you?"

"I have only one in mind. But let us have your three."

"No, give me your one first."

"There is only one for me; that is Michael Rua."

"Yes, it is true; he has been my right hand from the start."

"More than your right hand, your head and your heart; there could be no-one else."

Nothing more was said: they both knew what was in question; Don Bosco was grateful to Don Cagliero for absolving him from having to make a choice, a choice which could only have been between Cagliero himself and Rua.

The First Bishop

In November 1883, the Holy See issued two important documents; one appointed Don Giovanni Cagliero as Provicar Apostolic of Western and Northern Patagonia and Don Fagnano, Prefect Apostolic of Southern Patagonia, Tierra del Fuego (the land of fire!). Don Cagliero was not raised to the episcopal rank, though this was expected to come later. Don Bosco talked the matter over with Cardinal Alimonda and with the Cardinal Bini who was the official 'Protector' of the Salesian Society in Rome. Both supported his plea that the episcopate be awarded before Cagliero set off again. With only the implacable Cardinal Ferrieri (champion of Mgr. Gastaldi) opposing, Pope Leo in October 1884, agreed "to give the episcopal office direct to the new Provicar Apostolic of Patagonia".

It was a happy day for Don Bosco. His thoughts went back to that day when the fatherless boy first stood with him at the door; he was thirteen but so small that when Mamma Margaret objected there was no room for him, Don Bosco laughed, "Well, this fellow is so small that we can string him up from the rafters in a bird cage!" (Others said "It was an onion bag!" No matter.) Well, he wasn't small now, but a strapping, vigorous man. This was the sick boy, near to dying, over whose head anxious bronze giants had gathered, with the dove that dropped an olive branch over his head. Now the 'vision' was coming into reality, with Cagliero today a healthy forty-six.

The episcopal consecration took place in the sanctuary of Valdocco on December 7th, 1884, a memorable occasion. During the solemn procession, Mgr. Cagliero saw his eighty year old mother standing; he went at once to her and kissing her white head, escorted her to the seat of honour reserved for her. At the end, it was to Don Bosco that he turned, offering him, 'his' Don Bosco, the first kiss on his episcopal ring.

Don Rua Official Vicar General of the Society

Two months earlier, Don Bosco had proposed to his Superior Chapter that Don Rua be appointed his Vicar General with full responsibility, which was at once accepted by the Chapter, and by the Pope, at the beginning of December that year.

The Episcopal Palace a Wooden Hut

Bishop Cagliero left Turin for South America in February 1885, taking with him eighteen Salesians and six Salesian Sisters. At home Don Bosco waited with eager expectation the long, interesting letters that, from time to time, the Bishop could send him. They were immediately given to the *Salesian Bulletin* for publication.

By the middle of 1886, Cagliero was able to report that the whole of the more populated western area of Patagonia had been visited and catechised by Salesian missionaries. "In the immense valley of Chichinal, we have baptized 1,700 Indians after six hours a day instructing them in the Catholic religion. My episcopal 'palace' is a fine wooden hut, with dried mud between the rough planks to keep out the rain. There are no beds but our good Indian friends have given us warm skins to lie on."

He describes later a long journey across the continent of 1,500 kilometres during which they administered 997 baptisms, blessed 101 marriages and confirmed 1,513. It was while the party was crossing the Cordigliera range, which rises to 10,000 feet, that the Bishop's horse took fright and bolted on a narrow mountain road. Cagliero threw himself off but was badly hurt and bruised, with two broken ribs. He was laid up in primitive conditions for three weeks, before completing the journey from the Atlantic to the Pacific Ocean.

Chapter Forty-Two

THE CLOSING YEARS, THE LONG MEMORIES

NOT FOR NOTHING did Don Bosco take the gentle Saint Francis de Sales as his patron and model, someone to curb his own at times impetuous reactions to injustice; from his childhood he was always ready to fight for what he thought right. His devotion to St. Francis undoubtedly helped him throughout his life; but in his closing years, it became especially noticeable. In spite of trials and problems, he became, possibly like all old people at the end of their days, less troubled in mind. He would leave more to God: like St. Francis, he now seemed to be able to "walk through the raindrops without getting wet". There was a gentleness, a peace about him, a benevolence towards even those who hurt him.

Now worn out, having perforce to rest in the shade and talk to such of his sons who might visit him, he had time to look back over the years. Names came to him. The first Oratory, the dear priests who had helped him in so many ways; Don Cafasso, Don Borel, Don Alassonati, who came with his breviary under his arm. His wonderful Mamma Margaret, of course. The first boys, the young Garelli with whom he had said the first "Hail Mary" that began it all. The eight year old Michael Rua, Cagliero, of course, Pietro Enria, Buzzetti, the faithful one. But there had been plenty of priests and Brothers and boys since the early days. Why, who was that boy who came with his books of sins? Only the other day, wasn't it?

Hard Pavements and Books of Sins

It was in the beginning of the new term, October 1886, that the fourteen year old Luigi Orione had been accepted at Valdocco. His father worked on street pavements and young Luigi had often to kneel by his side chipping the stones and fitting them in. At the Oratory, he was fascinated by all he saw of Don Bosco and on the rare occasions now when the old priest could come down to the playground, he made sure to get as near as he could to him. Don Bosco spotted him.

"What have we here, a new boy? Where do you come from?" Luigi told him.

"Oh, is the moon as big there as it is in Turin?" Luigi laughed and thought it was.

Though Don Bosco was always ready to hear confessions, his weakness restricted them greatly; only boys preparing for the Novitiate were allowed to go to him but Luigi, though a junior, begged to be allowed to go just once. Permission was granted. He at once began to prepare himself for this momentous event by getting a book on confession from the library and writing down his sins. Apart from one or two of the greater ones, like murder and suicide, he decided he had pretty well committed the lot. Soon one exercise book was filled, then a second, then a third. Don Bosco was sitting in a chair and Luigi knelt at his feet.

"Give me your sins, Luigi." He took the first book, held it in his hand as if to weigh it and then tore it up. He treated the second in the same way and likewise the third. "Now you have confessed all your sins; they are forgiven, forget all about them!" After the absolution, he smiled at Luigi, a smile the boy never forgot. "Remember, Luigi, you and I are always going to be friends, always."

Perhaps he saw something in Luigi that he had seen in Dominic Savio or in Michael Rua, this Luigi Orione, the great priest who founded the Order of the Sons of Divine Providence, and the Little Sisters of Charity, caring for the young and the old, for the sick, the incurable, the "outcasts of this world, trying to love those whom nobody loves". Don Orione was beatified on October 26th, 1980.

Then there was the other day when he was trying to talk to the Sisters, his voice so weak that Don Bonetti had to act as a sort of loudspeaker for him. "Tell them Our Lady is here, amongst them," he whispered. "Don Bosco says Our Lady is your mother and protects you," Don Bonetti explained. "No, no, I want to tell them that the Madonna is here, in this house and is pleased with them." Don Bonetti made of that, "Don Bosco says that if you are good, the Madonna will be pleased with you". Don Bosco made a last effort. "No, no, I am trying to say that the Madonna is here, in this house, with you in person, and She covers it with her protecting mantle." He hoped they had understood at last.

Then there was that very old Countess Uggucioni, who had done so much for him, whom he met by chance when he was being helped out of the train in Florence. She was just as infirm. "Oh, my dear Countess, how are you? Would you like to dance?" "Oh, Don Bosco, see what a state we are both in!" "Never mind," he laughed, "we shall dance in heaven!"

A few years ago, there was that rather short, earnest, scholarly young priest who came to see him in Valdocco, to ask him a few questions. After talking for half an hour, Don Bosco said he had a meeting of his Rectors and would not be able to show him round the House; but just treat it as his own and go where he wanted and then come into lunch. The priest was Achille Ratti, who, fifty-one years later, was to speak often about that meeting with a saint; he it was who, as Pope Pius XI, canonised Don Bosco on that April day in 1934, before 300,000 in St. Peter's Square, crying their "Viva Don Bosco!" as his boys had done. But that was perhaps not given to the old priest to know just then, not even in his dreams.

Chapter Forty-Three
AT DAWN INTO THE LIGHT

THE DUKE OF Norfolk, a staunch Catholic, greatly revered Don Bosco and was always happy to see him. His visit in 1885 and the circumstances surrounding it, is given prominence in the official history of the Society. In May 1887, he called again on his way to Rome and discussed the proposed opening of Salesian work in England. He stayed for lunch with the community and although he used French in writing to or speaking with Don Bosco, he would find many to converse with him at table.

All that year of 1887, Don Bosco was failing daily. The last time he went out seems to be on October 2nd. His carriage brought him through the playground to the steps leading to his rooms. The boys greeted him with affection and some of the older ones helped him up the stairs, with many stops for him to get his breath. He could gasp out a laugh, "If anybody has any bellows to spare, I'd like to borrow them; mine seem to be full of holes!"

In November, the three Salesians who were to inaugurate the first of Don Bosco's works for the English-speaking world, his last personal foundation, came to ask his blessing. They were Father Edward McKiernan, Father Charles Macey and an Italian Brother who did not persevere. They arrived in London on November 16th and were met by Father Francis Bourne, another of Don Bosco's English friends. At one time, he wanted to join Don Bosco in Turin, who, however, advised him to stay where he was. He eventually became Cardinal Archbishop of Westminster .

As the year moved into winter, the candle seemed to be burning out. Mass was possible, supported by a priest, on December 5th and 6th; on the 11th, he could not finish; it was his last, from June 5th, 1841.

Weeks before Don Rua had sent an urgent cable to Bishop Cagliero: "Papa alarming collapse" which brought the Bishop as fast as ships could speed him. He arrived on December 7th, greeted with emotional affection by Don Bosco who ignoring his own troubles, was at once solicitous to know if the Bishop had recovered from his accident and broken ribs. They spoke for a couple of hours; then Cagliero asked Don Bosco to hear his confession, another 'last' of so many over the years. What was said to him, he wrote down and kept.

All his life, Don Bosco had spoken of confession, the Sacrament of Reconciliation, to his boys, even more than the Mass and Communion, much though he encouraged even daily Communion. Confession implying sorrow for sins, implying willingness to turn back to God, to trust in His love and mercy, was for him perhaps the most important part of every priest's ministry. So in the last days, quite literally at his last gasp, he would hear some confessions.

On December 17th, thirty boys, due to enter the novitiate, were admitted singly to his room; they knelt at his side, something they would never forget.

A collapse followed and on December 31st, all the Last Sacraments were administered. But the guttering candle flared up again and for three weeks there was a surprising recovery. On January 13th, the Duke of Norfolk was in Rome and heard of Don Bosco's grave illness. He at once hurried to Turin and, Earl Marshal of England though he was, knelt humbly at the bedside for half an hour. They spoke, he said, of the London Salesians, now two months in Battersea, of the Chinese Missions, and of Ireland, a country always dear to Don Bosco's heart. He would kiss the dying priest's hand as he blessed him.

On January 21st, the recovery ended; there could be no further hope. Don Bosco was dying as the saints die, happy to be going to God, concerned about his sons, who would have to carry on. "There are still debts on the Sacro Cuore; what will my Salesians think of me leaving them all these debts?" There was a last thought for his boys, for the thousands of boys who had passed through his hands. "Tell my boys that I shall be waiting for them in Paradise." It was seen as the fulfilment of his promise after his illness of 1846, when many of them had prayed night and day for his recovery. For a further ten days he lingered. He was suffering, unable to change his position. One of the priests suggested, "Dear Father, think of Our Lord on the cross, suffering, too, and unable to move." "Yes, I am doing that all the time." Shortly after midnight, now the 31st, it was plain he was entering into his final 'agony'. Don Rua watching and praying, at last put on his stole and began the prayers for the dying. They were all there on their knees, the weeping Buzzetti, Pietro Enria, Viglietti, his secretary and others. When Bishop Cagliero arrived, Don Rua passed over the stole to him. He bent over the bed and said clearly, "Don Bosco, we are all here, your sons. We want to tell you how sorry we are for ever causing you any pain. We ask you to give us your last blessing. I will raise your arm and say the words for you." The blessing was for all Salesians, past and present, far and near.

As the dawn began to break in that wintry sky, the breathing stopped. The Bishop said slowly the prayer Don Bosco had taught him and the others to say as the last before going to sleep at night: "Jesus, Mary and Joseph, I give you my heart and my soul, Jesus, Mary and Joseph, assist me in my last agony, Jesus, Mary and Joseph, may I breathe forth my soul in peace with you". It was 4.45 a.m. He took off the stole and put it round Don Bosco's shoulders, as Pietro Enria gently closed the eyes that had no further need of light for he had already passed into Light Eternal.

Chapter Forty-Four
EPILOGUE

Of all great hearts, the greatest is still the heart of a saint.
G. K. Chesterton.

FOR SAINTS, FORTUNATELY, there is no scale of measurement. It would be a pity if there were; the question simply does not arise. One thing is certain. There were no greater men or women in the nineteenth century than the saints who gave it its true glory. History offers us its great figures on many stages: men of war, men of science, of medicine, of art, of engineering, of politics, with women as great in their own, usually gentler, spheres. Many of them gave their lives to improve the lot of their fellow men. But none gave more than the saints. They were totally committed, their moral integrity unclouded; unlike many of the historically great, they had no 'private lives,' no honours, no fortune. They were ambitious only for the spread of God's work for the good of mankind; for themselves they were completely disinterested.

John Bosco was born two months after the defeat of Napoleon at Waterloo; he would sometimes describe himself as "an old grenadier of Waterloo". Napoleon made many contributions to humanity in law, in science, in history but his fame as a great man rests paramountly on his undoubted military prowess. It was his insatiable ambition that drove him to his many conquests, conquests that made all Europe a graveyard, brought tragedy and misery to countless homes in every country.

St. John Bosco, and such as St. John Cottolengo, Luigi Orione, dried the tears of orphans, brought solace to the old and the sick, gave shelter to the poor and education to generations. School histories tell our children of the greatness of such as Napoleon: they say nothing of John Bosco. But wherein does greatness lie? In the warmakers or in the peacemakers? There can be no doubt, "sub specie aeternitatis," in the eyes of God, where it lies.

Don Bosco left behind him two new religious Societies, to which God gave unusual growth. May we in all humility record that for the first hundred years of their joint existence, the Salesians and the Salesian Sisters together opened 2,600 Houses, that is, an average of one new foundation every two weeks for a hundred years. God gave the increase, God it is who calls every worker to His service, glory to God for entrusting to Don Bosco's sons and daughters a share in the mystery of salvation.

In the aftermath of the Second World War, the rise of atheistic Marxism in Eastern Europe, in the Far East, in China, Viet Nam, and in recent years in certain parts of Africa, has cost the Salesians some 200 Houses. But losses have been more than made up, notably, it must be said, outside 'Western' lands. The Holy Spirit has been active to an ever greater degree in such areas as India, with its six expanding Provinces, already sending splendid missionaries to Africa and elsewhere from its almost 2,000 Salesians. Poland, too, in spite of its political situation, with four Provinces and over 1,000 Salesians, is also sending missionaries for Africa, sparing them from its many-sided activities radiating from more than 140 parishes. Precise statistics are obsolete before they can be printed, but in any case, mere numbers are of little importance. What matters is that God should continue to use the simple, unpretentious spirit and charism of St. John Bosco to further His work in the four corners of the earth.

Blessed be GOD!

In writing of the great works of the saints, especially of those such as Saint John Bosco who worked for the poor, let us put in a word for our faltering humanity. Had it not been for the generosity of rich and poor, some of the rich almost impoverishing themselves, some of the poor giving to others scarcely more in need than themselves, and for the traditionally generous middle classes, Don Bosco could not have fed a single hungry child, nor built a school, an orphanage, a church, and what we say of Don Bosco, we say of all the saints who have spent their lives in bringing for the love of God, solace and comfort to their fellowman. That humanity continues its generosity today.

Let us pray that, in the final count, God, giving glory to His saints, may include in His infinite mercy, all those who helped them attain to that glory. We may be sure that He will.

SUMMARY

Giovanni (John) Melchiore Bosco born August 16th, 1815.
Ordained priest in Turin, June 5th, 1841.
Foundation of Salesian Society, December 18th, 1859.
Foundation of Sisters, Daughters of Mary Help of Christians, August 5th, 1872.
Death of Don Bosco, January 31st, 1888.
Beatification, June 2nd, 1929.
Canonisation, Easter Sunday, April 1st, 1934.
Canonisation, Mother Mary D. Mazzarello, June 24th, 1951.
Canonisation, Dominic Savio, June 12th, 1954.
Canonisation, Joseph Cafasso, June 22nd, 1947.
Beatification, Michael Rua, October 29th, 1972.
Beatification, Bishop L. Versiglia, Martyr, May 15th, 1983.
Beatification, Father C. Caravario, Martyr, May 15th, 1983.
Beatification, D. Philip Rinaldi, April 29th, 1990.

M[illegible]s

I[illegible]ership Flies

by

David L Cox

First Edition

Published by David L Cox
PO Box 28
Lichfield
Staffs WS14 0LD
England

Fax No: UK: 0543 481815
International: +44 543 481815

August 1993

Printed by Tresises,
Burton-on-Trent and Derby

ISBN 0-9513472-2-5

ACKNOWLEDGEMENT

With thanks to Sven Atterhed for first introducing me to the story of 'fleas in boxes', pages 1 to 4.

If ....

you put fleas in a box and close the lid, they jump about, hurting themselves by banging on the walls and the ceiling:

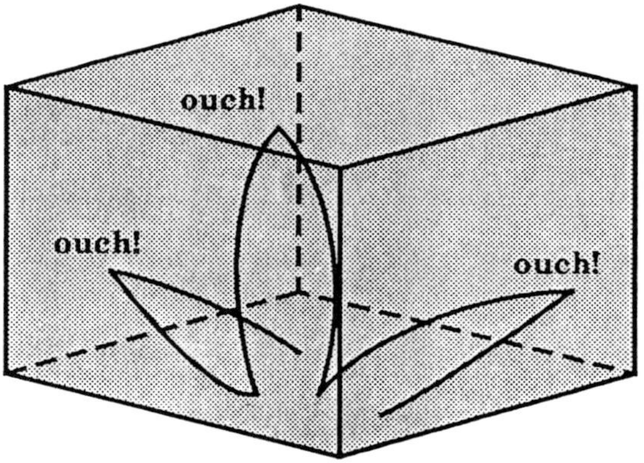

After a time, they realise what is causing the pain, after which they jump around just within the confines of the box:

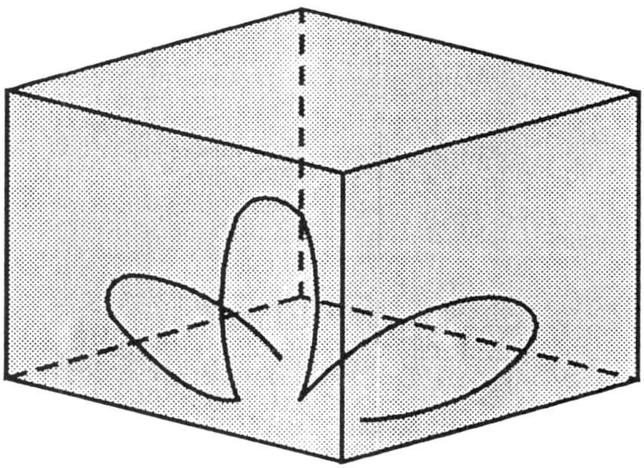

If the box is then removed - guess what happens.

The fleas continue jumping around within the confines of where the box was:

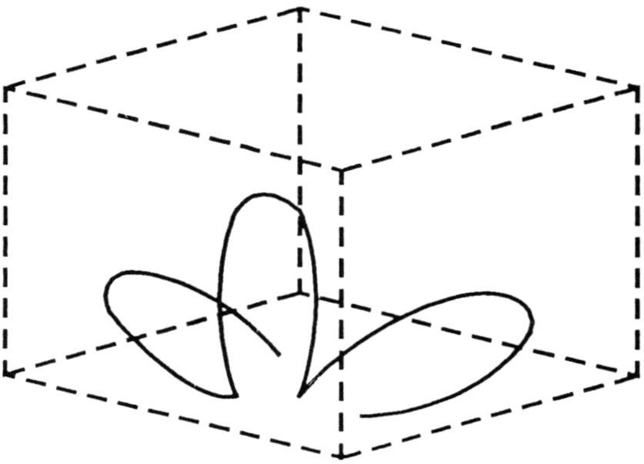

We are all trained fleas .....

CONTENTS

And in the beginning there were ....

Section I

Fleas in Boxes

1. Introducing Fred and His Friends

Fred is a management flea.

He has his own box all to himself.

Fred in His Box

His colleagues also have their own individual boxes, all to themselves.

Let's introduce you to five of them including Ben, Fred's boss:

Attila Ben Charlie Dennis Eric

It took Fred some time to understand how the confines of his box, and those of his colleagues, were drawn. It was by 'management instruments' such as rules, procedures, job descriptions and policies.

For example

- the Car Policy says that Fred can have a two litre car - what it is actually saying is that Fred can't have a three litre car

- the Attendance Hours Policy says that Fred's hours of work are nine to five - what it is actually saying is that they can't be eight to four, or ten to six

- the Capital Authorisation Procedure required that Fred needed Ben's signature on the appropriate form before he could even request spending any capital at all.

And, of course, reporting relationships were clearly defined, which spelt out the limits of the freedom each flea had.

This was emphasised by the way the pictures were drawn of the organisation:

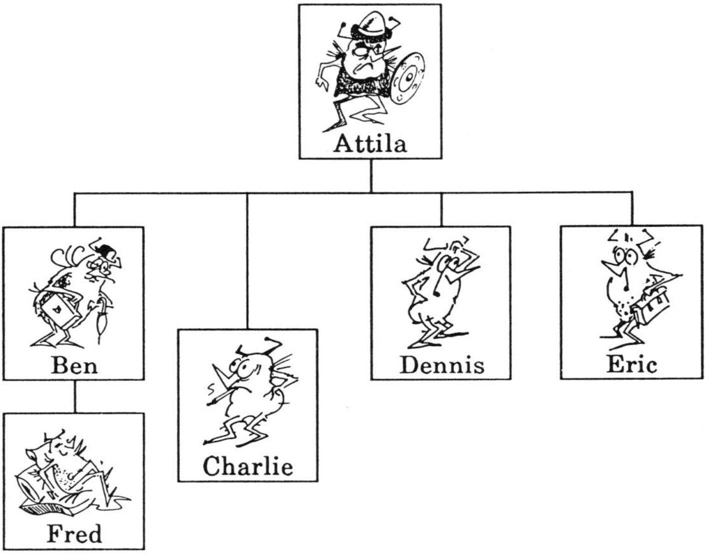

You could tell that Charlie wasn't as important a flea as Ben, Dennis and Eric, because his box was always drawn a little further away from Attila's than theirs.

Moreover, you could suspect that no two fleas did anything together. Attila told Ben what to do, and Ben told Fred what to do. Ben and Charlie can only relate through Attila.

Bigger fleas have smaller fleas
To fetch and carry for 'em
And smaller fleas have other fleas
And so ad infinitum

2. Breeding Fleas

Why do organisations apparently revel in drawing more boxes with fleas in?

'Revel' was the word which sprang to Fred's mind, because it seemed that his organisation, to which Fred had belonged for several years, was always doing so.

Only a couple of years ago, for instance, there had been a reorganisation of Dennis the Flea's part of the 'flea circus'. This had added more boxes with what could only be described as smaller fleas in them:

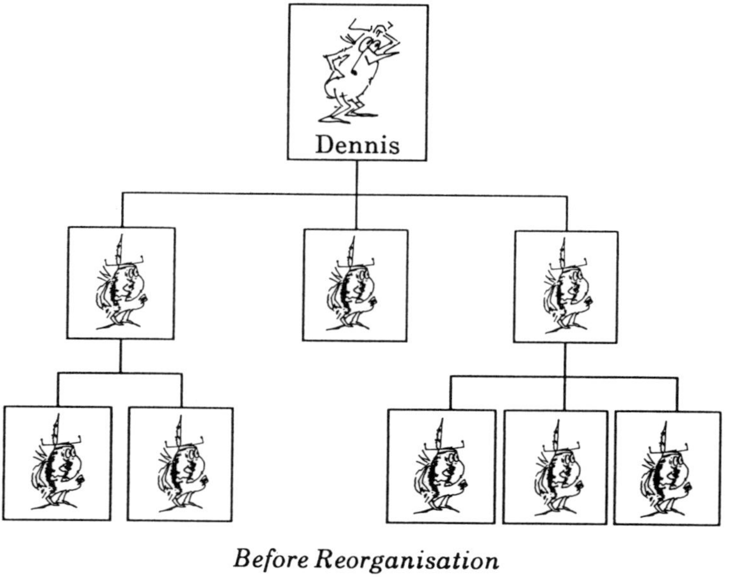

Before Reorganisation

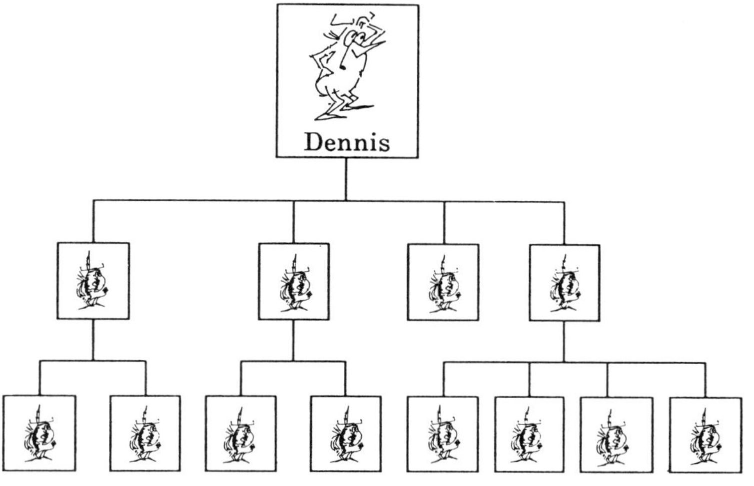

After Reorganisation

It wasn't as if there was any apparent good business reason for the changes - Dennis's overall responsibilities were largely as before.

It dawned on Fred that basically the reason why such reorganisations occurred (rather than 'were needed') was as an outcome of experiential learning. Fleas had been trained to behave in this way, and were rewarded for doing so.

Your importance as a flea was proportional to the number of fleas that you could convince the organisation you needed below you, the size of your revenue budget and the like.

As a result, your status was recognised not only by the relative size of your salary (you hoped - you never saw anyone else's) but also by the size of your office and desk, the thickness of your carpet, the type of car parking space you were allocated, the sort of title you could have, where you could eat and which toilets you could use.

The effects of what Fred realised was an insidious process were there for all to see.

Office shelves groaned with policy and procedural manuals. Functional specialists abounded - fleas with titles which included the descriptions 'Corporate', 'Administration', 'Personnel' and 'Management Services'. There were even the odd esoteric flea collections called 'Operational Research', 'Organisations and Methods', 'Industrial Relations' (relations with industries??) and 'Customer Complaints'.

Customers! Now there's a thing - customers, who Fred knew intuitively were pretty important to the success of the business, were only recognised organisationally by the fleas as complainants.

YOU MIGHT BE OUR BIGGEST CUSTOMER SIR BUT YOUR ALSO THE BIGGEST PAIN IN OUR ... ©x!Δxx!

3. The Fleas and Devolution

Fairly recently Fred, and all of the other fleas in the organisation, had had a surprise.

Attila had called them all together and announced "Devolution". Fred and the rest were all to be let out of their boxes (or at least, that's how Fred interpreted it), and were to be "empowered". The organisation, Attila said, wanted them to 'contribute to business aims with more freedom than they had ever previously imagined possible'.

The announcement took a whole day, and was supported by outside experts. It was very professionally done, with glossy hand-outs.

All the fleas felt good about the trust that Attila was talking about investing in them.

Within a month, it was as if nothing had happened! All the fleas were back behaving as they always had. This worried Fred considerably - because he realised that he was a highly trained flea like the rest, and unless he or some other flea did something about it, he was captive in his box *even though it was no longer there* (apparently).

Fred before devolution

Fred after devolution

Fred decided to 'have a go'.

He started jumping outside his box - or rather where it had been. To his delight, he found that he actually had more freedom than he had assumed. It was as if having jumped out of his box - his 'comfort zone' where he knew he was safe - there was a sort of 'neutral zone' around it where his activities were at least tolerated. He started to build some very fruitful alliances with fleas whom he had never directly related to before, for instance those outside his boss-flea Ben's part of the structure.

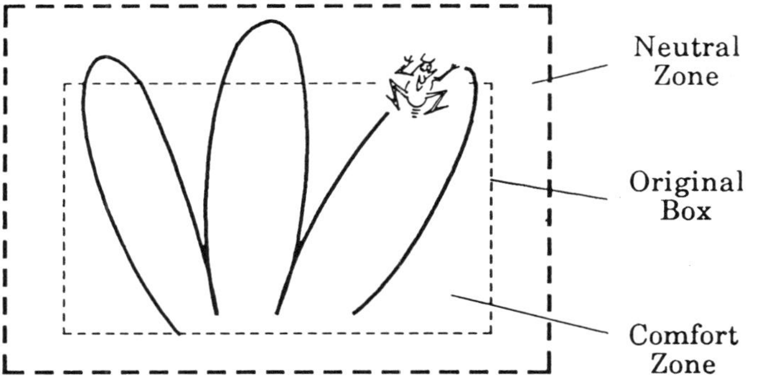

Fred jumping into his 'neutral zone'

He was feeling good about his new effectiveness, and jumped further and further until one day - zap! He got into real trouble, and was disciplined by Ben for having interfered in areas which were outside his responsibility (i.e. outside his original box).

What Fred had done, of course, was travel into the danger zone - or rather for fleas, the 'swat zone'.

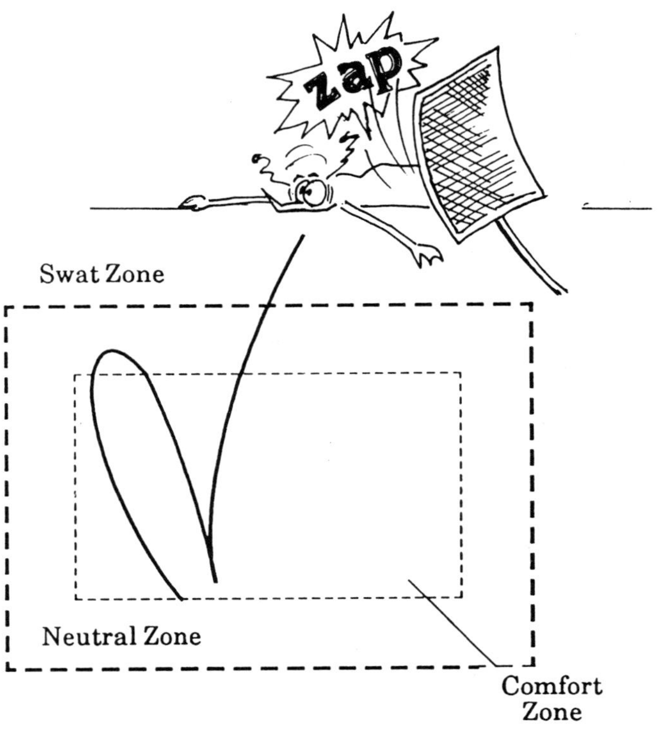

He retreated into where his original box had been - his comfort zone, blooded but hopefully unbowed.

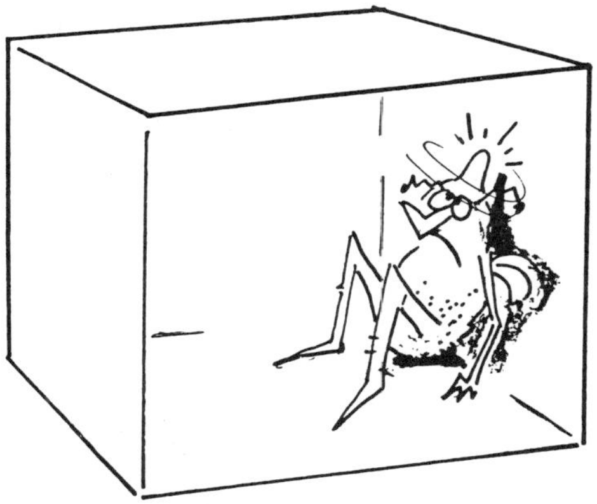

All of the other 'devolved' fleas had been watching Fred, and his fate had reinforced their belief that whatever people said, including Attila making big announcements about 'Devolution', they weren't going to leave their boxes voluntarily.

And that's why the Devolution announcement achieved nothing.

Attila himself, of course, had retreated to his comfort zone - his Big Flea box, for the same reasons as all the other fleas.

AH'TTILA YOU
COME SEE HOW WE JAPAN FLEA
DO IT. EH!

4. Big Flea Attila Visits Japan

After the devolution episode had passed, the fleas had another surprise. They heard that Attila was to visit Japan. No-one knew why - why should they - it was nothing to do with them what Big Fleas chose to do.

What was happening was this.

Attila was the only flea who knew that the organisation was in trouble - that's why he had tried devolution. He *would* be the only one who knew, of course. He was the only one with all of the necessary information - one of the classic ways of keeping fleas in their boxes is to limit the information available to them. Even Ben, Charlie, Dennis and Eric didn't have it all - they only knew the bits that they individually supplied to Attila.

Attila had decided, that given the problems he saw the organisation had, he would visit Japan, because the Japanese had all the answers to corporate success - or so the legend went.

Attila returned and immediately initiated what everyone thought was a brilliant idea (cheers for Attila - he always had the best ideas! - one of the reasons why he was Big Flea).

Quality circles - that was it. Several were to be formed, to examine such topics as Product Range, Market Positioning, Competitor Strengths and Weaknesses, Just in Time Technologies and the like. Volunteer fleas would form the circles - teams of fleas who would be an adjunct to the mainstream organisation. They would be given the greatest of freedom to conduct their tasks,and be given the necessary time and resources.

Well, the fleas volunteered in swarms (or whatever is the collective noun for fleas). They worked for weeks in their circles, stealing as much time as possible - including what used to be, very strictly, 'their own time' (that is, outside the hours of nine to five). They loved every minute of this freedom - and came up with some wonderful ideas, much to their surprise.

The day came when they made presentations to the 'Top Flea' panel - Attila, plus Ben, Charlie, Dennis and Eric. The presentations went like a dream - the Quality Circle fleas were so pleased to have made what they saw were important suggestions for improving the business.

Off they then went, back to their boxes, waiting expectantly for Attila to announce changes as a result of their recommendations.

Guess what happened? Yes, nothing. Their ideas had, inevitably, challenged the very basis on which the organisational relationships were built. The Top Fleas found many ways to articulate why the ideas would not work. They would, wouldn't they, being the most highly conditioned (sorry - trained) fleas of all, with the most to lose if things changed?

I KNOW IT SEEMS A GOOD IDEA, OLD BOY
BUT TAKE IT FROM ME - IT JUST WOULDN'T
WORK IN OUR ORGANISATION

5. Flea Diseases

The fleas in the organisation settled back down to business as usual after the failed experiments of devolution and quality circles - even though the fleas had come to understand during those experiments that the organisation was in trouble.

Fred clearly understood by now why they had all settled back down - the fleas had been trained to jump around in their boxes - their comfort zones, outside of which they all knew was at best a limited neutral zone, outside of which was the dreaded swat zone.

He amused himself by reinforcing this understanding with the concept of megalomania and sycophancy.

The disease of megalomania takes hold over time when management fleas continually punish subordinate fleas (i.e. keep knocking them back into their boxes) who question their ideas and instructions, to the point where the challenges cease: the belief that one is always right - megalomania - being the result.

The same process in reverse produces sycophancy: after being subjected to pain for long enough every time one voices an opinion, subordinate fleas retreat

into their comfort zones, cease to challenge ever again, and always do as they are told.

"The deadly duopoly of the Megalomaniac - Sycophant bond" was how Fred christened his thoughts.

Naturally, all the management fleas operate in both roles.

Except, that is, for Attila himself, who has no sycophant role within the organisation. Indeed, neither does he have peers, who even in the most rigid of flea-box organisations can occasionally help to stop the onset of megalomania. No wonder the Attilas of this world seem more prone to succumb to megalomania - and isn't it worse even than that? Their pre-eminent position of relatively unchallenged power allows them to live their own personal ambitions through the organisations they lead, invariably and eventually to the detriment of those organisations.

Section II

Performing Fleas

FREDS
GREAT
ESCAPE
PLAN

1. Fred the Learning Flea

Fred had not been wasting his time since he came to understand that he was a trained flea like the rest.

Indeed, he had resolved to escape from his box: his personal mission no less! He would have to work out how to achieve this mission.

His first and crucial step was to start changing what was between his ears - the most difficult change he would *ever* face. He had to learn, and indeed relearn, new skills, new knowledge, new attitudes, new values.

This process had begun some time ago, through observation: seeing fleas breeding for no apparent good business reason, the failed devolution, the aborted introduction of Quality Circles, and his conclusions about megalomania and sycophancy.

He had supplemented this learning in a variety of ways.

He began reading the latest ideas on managing flea circuses and particularly why fleas behave the way they do. He attended several management flea conferences and seminars.

He also went on as many management flea courses as he was allowed. Interestingly, this was one example of how he learned to use - *to manipulate* - his existing environment to help him achieve his personal mission. If you were a well-behaved flea at Fred's level, one of the 'prizes' was that you were allowed to attend up to two weeks of courses at Business Schools per year. More 'important' fleas were allowed more.

Most fleas never used their allocation.

There were two reasons for this. Firstly, the fleas were worried that whilst they were away, their flea-boxes would be attacked. Secondly, that this 'flea-dip' approach to training never had any effect - as soon as they returned from a training course, what they had learned was soon forgotten because it never seemed to relate to the workplace.

He was also into action learning - testing his new skills and knowledge by trying them out in his day-to-day activities and learning from the results. This proved enormously effective.

It taught him that he gained his greatest motivation from achieving what he set out to do, however small: "Win today's match, and you can't wait to go out and win tomorrow's". Through involving the fleas who reported to him, he found that they equally responded to winning as a motivator, *especially*

YOU'RE SURE THAT KEY WILL REOPEN
OUR BOXES ARE YOU CHARLIE ?

Working together ...

... at play ...

... and at home ...

where they had contributed equally and fully with Fred in deciding 'how the game was to be played'.

Moreover, it taught Fred that collectively the group of them - he hesitated at this point to call them a team - came up with better ideas than he could possibly have devised on his own.

As these 'experiments' progressed, Fred realised that his attitudes, through adopting new values, were changing, and that new relationships were developing between him and his fleas. He was even getting feedback from them - they were obviously responding to the openness Fred had started to create. They were even telling him some home truths about himself that they would not have dared to do in the past.

Fred was finding this whole experience challenging and positive on the one hand - but there was no doubt he was also feeling very uncomfortable on occasion.

But then he would, wouldn't he? He was into unknown territory outside his box.

"There's no gain without pain" rang in his ears, and the word 'humility' had entered his vocabulary.

Up to this point, Fred had controlled the action - learning activities in such a way that they were not visible outside his own area of responsibility - not visible especially to Ben. He didn't want to get swatted again!

However, the time had come when Fred had learned as much as he felt he needed from covert action-learning 'games' with his reportees.

He decided what his next step was to be, and he needed Ben's support and approval for it. That was not going to be easy to earn.

2. Fred the Quality Flea

"Quality is meeting agreed customer expectations."

"Your customers are not only external - they are also internal - your boss, your colleagues, your subordinates."

"Use selling and marketing techniques, with *all* of your customers."

Fred had been introduced to such concepts on one of the courses he had attended.

He had found some initial difficulties in understanding them, but his successes through action-learning had helped. For instance, his subordinate-customer-fleas had responded to being fully involved in and winning 'games' together; subordinate - customer - flea needs being satisfied, needs which he had not considered before, needs which had not been allowed to surface in the bureaucratic environment he was used to.

And so to selling his plan to Ben.

Fred researched as fully as possible what his customer-boss-flea Ben's needs-wants-expectations were. He analysed which of these he, Fred, felt he was best at satisfying. He identified how he could best package and sell (i.e. how he should present) his product (i.e. his plan) to Ben using the information from his analysis.

He was much encouraged as he went through this process, as he had found a basis for establishing a strong correlation between what some of Ben's needs were, and what the plan he wanted Ben to approve could satisfy. He felt a willing buyer existed for his product, and he had his marketing strategy in place.

Now he only had to get his timing right.

Fred learned another lesson at this point. Folklore had it that there are some fleas who always seem to be lucky in life, and some unlucky. Instead, the truth is that the apparently 'lucky' ones are the ones who are ready to take opportunities when, inevitably, they fleetingly appear.

It happened thus: Fred was ready just before Attila had announced his initiative of Quality Circles following his visit to Japan. The way Fred wanted to progress his idea, as we shall see later, was in line with the thinking behind Quality Circles. How could Ben at that moment reject even only a subordinate flea wishing to take his own initiative in support of Attila's?

So Ben gave Fred the go-ahead, at least for Stage 1 of his 'product', at which point a progress report would be needed to trigger any possible Stage 2.

Fred was just a bit pleased with himself and the way he had applied his newly-learned skills. For instance, he had constructed his presentation in a way which purposely portrayed his ideas as *significant*, and *complex*: *significant*, so that Ben's ego was 'stroked' (it's no good wasting the time of an important flea on insignificant matters); and *complex*, just enough so that Ben couldn't understand it all, and wouldn't expose his ignorance by asking questions on the technicalities.

"Don't present big fleas with Bicycle Sheds, even big ones, to approve. They understand Bicycle Sheds."

He had manipulated Ben successfully by having prepared himself so well in understanding the customer's needs, and then meeting them.

"The quality standard is Right First Time."

Zero defects so far!

Fred at this point pondered about the swat zone. He had certainly strayed into it in his presentation to Ben, but hadn't been swatted.

Another lesson learned! The swat zone is not rigid - it retreats if the right circumstances are created. The neutral zone is expandable: space can be "grabbed".

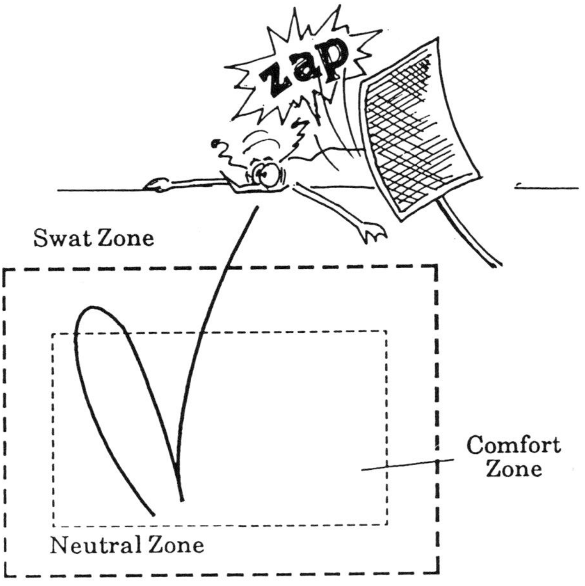

Fred's original experience with the swat zone.

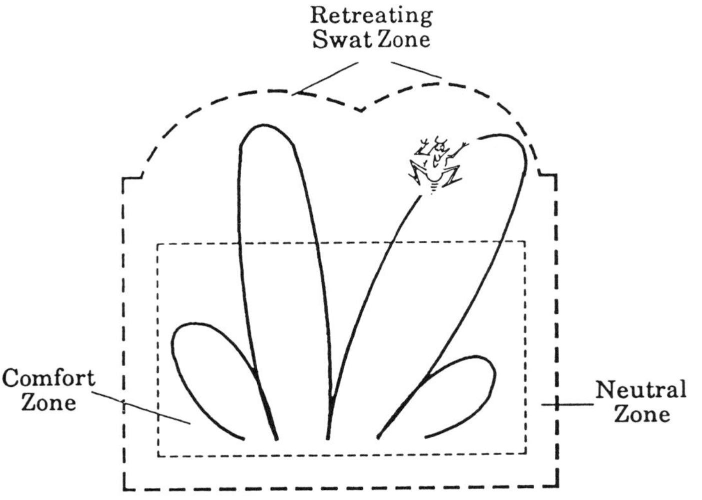

Fred forces the swat zone to retreat

B

3. Ben the Corporate Flea

In selling his product to Ben, Fred had been clever - but not as clever as he thought. He had certainly correctly identified enough of Ben's needs to have got past go, but had not identified the key one.

You see, Ben was a wily - even fly - old flea. He had been with the organisation for many years, years full of experiential flea-box learning, learning devoted to his overriding personal ambition: survival as a corporate flea.

Ben had never strayed - sorry jumped - even near his swat zone. He had never experimented, nor taken risks. As a consequence, he had never made mistakes from which to learn and naturally had never achieved anything of significance for the organisation, all matters which are at this juncture beside the point.

The only time he ever got excited and passionate was when other fleas got too close to his box. Over the years, fewer and fewer of them had even attempted this, partly because he became more astute in seeing them advancing a long way off and deflecting them from a distance; and partly because he had built up his role in such a way that it was perceived that only he could do it. In other words he had strengthened the fabric of his box.

BENS BOX
KEEP OUT

Among his several supporting survival strategies was: to be selective in his relationships. He always chose to be close to those who were seen to be organisationally in favour, especially the ones with clout - and of course drop them when this condition ceased to be met. Another strategy, linked to the first, was to encourage the loyalty to himself personally of as many of the management fleas throughout the organisation as possible. For instance, whenever promising junior fleas were promoted, he went out of his way to have them believe he had played a key part behind the scenes in their success.

All in all, his modus operandi was to back those winners who could help him survive, and drop the losers who couldn't - very focused, and he did it very well.

Now to Attila and Ben.

Attila had been a colleague of Ben's for many years - they started in the organisation together. Attila was not like Ben at all. Attila was ambitious but often head-strong. He was always going to succeed until this weakness in his character led him to go too far.

Attila had been above all other fleas good for Ben (and vice versa), until now that is. Ben reasoned

IF I'M DROPPED LIKE A HOT POTATO I TRUST I CAN RELY ON YOUR SUPPORT GENTLEMEN!

that Attila was not going to survive for too much longer, he was becoming a loser. Ben could smell it. Ben started distancing himself from Attila, especially when the Devolution and Quality Circles initiatives came and failed.

On the other hand, Ben had to substitute this old alliance with others. He dismissed ones with Dennis and Eric - they weren't going anywhere.

Along had come Fred with his ideas. Obviously with Fred being only a middle-order flea, fostering Fred could not be a direct replacement for his ailing alliance with Attila. However, Ben reasoned, if Attila himself was vulnerable, there could be very turbulent and unpredictable times ahead and - who knows? - initiatives like Fred's could come in handy for Ben's continued personal survival plans. If not, so what - with all of his flea-box training, he would certainly know how to keep his distance from Fred and drop him like a hot potato if and when necessary.

And thus Ben, unbeknown to Fred, was manipulating him as a pawn in his personal survival game.

But, for the moment at least, this was of no consequence to Fred: Ben *had* approved his plan Stage 1.

HOWEVER GENTLEMEN WE HAVE DECIDED TO KEEP THE COMPANY CAT!

4. Agoraphobia Threatens Fred's Fleas

What Fred had sold to Ben, Stage 1, was to construct from scratch a new plan for his, Fred's, part of the business, *involving in its preparation his senior fleas fully.*

This sounded perhaps innocuous, but was not. Usually, "tablets of stone" descended from above which prescribed very thoroughly the parameters within which fleas like Fred could contribute, which precluded any possibility of original thought, and which certainly precluded subordinate flea participation. The words "SECRET" or "STRICTLY CONFIDENTIAL" were always etched into every tablet.

This time, the only constraints on Fred were that his plan had to be produced by a fixed date - 10 weeks hence - and that there was a maximum amount of money available that Fred could spend on its preparation.

Well, there was just *one* other caveat - that Fred was on his own: if this whole experiment went wrong, it was Fred's problem, not Ben's. This was a basis with which Fred was happy, because he knew that he was starting on what could be a long and winding individual and personal risk-taking road, and he wouldn't want it any other way from now on.

So, Fred got his top group of 10 or so fleas together. He told them that he had been very encouraged by their recent contributions to the action learning games, and their wish to be even more involved. He informed them that he had been very impressed with the ideas they had generated, and that he had made a note of some of the more significant ones. He went through this list, sufficient to demonstrate that what they added up to was a powerful glimpse of how they could develop the whole of Fred's part of the business in some very original ways.

Fred's fleas were impressed - of course with themselves! Their animated response, there and then, was to come up with even more ideas.

Fred let them talk for a while without taking part, and then pounced: here was his chance to break the megalomaniac:sycophant bond between himself and his subordinate fleas.

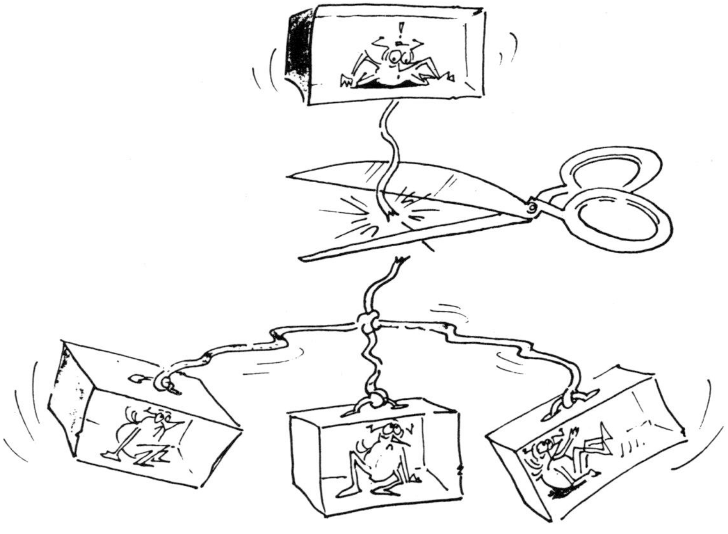

He said that he would like them to develop their ad hoc ideas into a complete Fred Business Plan, and that as they obviously didn't need him to help them, he wouldn't. Further, that in developing the plan, they could assume no constraints. Except one: time - Fred had to have their plan presented to him within 8 weeks (this would thus allow him two weeks after that to prepare a presentation to Ben). He added that if they needed resources, for instance money to be spent on off-site meeting locations, or the help of outside specialists, they only had to ask. (Fred knew they wouldn't ask for more than Ben had agreed to!).

He concluded by adding rather cheerily - "Any questions?" "See you in 8 weeks time".

The fleas became very excited by what Fred had said - "Wonderful", "What a challenge". Or at least, that was the response for the first few minutes. Then came the questions

" - What do you mean, no constraints?"
" - What do you mean - you won't be involved?"

Fred spent the next couple of hours arguing with his fleas, resisting their wish (although they didn't put it this way) for him to impose constraints - capital limitations, type of business, same buildings, same people and the like. He also had to argue why he, their leader, should *not* be involved in this, one of

the most important tasks on his job description - producing a business plan.

Fred successfully resisted both overtures. He would not construct a box around them in the form of Terms of Reference or Objectives, and he would not be part of the process - the sycophants would suffer agoraphobia and would not have the "guidance" of their megalomaniac to "help" them.

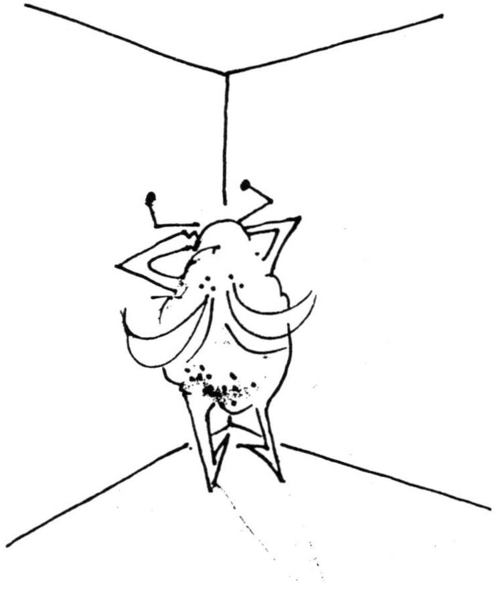

Ceremoniously, Fred left them to it.

Subsequently they let him know that they would be off site for a considerable part of the next 8 weeks and indeed gave him full details of where they would be and how they could be contacted.

He was to be left more or less alone running operations without them.

There were testing times ahead!

Would they break out of their sycophantic moulds? Could they withstand the strain of agoraphobia?

Would he be able to run operations without them? Would his tenuous deal with Ben withstand the inevitable squalls?

Would he be able to shield his fleas from the all-pervasive gaze of Attila, who despite Ben could be predicted to stop such anarchic experiments?

DID HE SAY, COME BACK IN 8 WEEKS
WITH SOME NEW IDEAS!

Fred's fleas plotting novel solutions in distant hotels ...

5. Developing Fleas

The 8 weeks allocated to the top group fleas to develop a Fred Business Plan started ticking away.

Week 1, day 2: Fred is walking around one of the more distant parts of his empire. This in itself was unusual - Fred usually stayed in the environs of his "conning tower", but felt that he must show his face with his top group fleas away as their junior fleas would be feeling lonely.

One such tenuously approaches Fred, and rather bravely asks Fred's advice on what is, to the junior flea, World War III breaking out in his section. Fred doesn't know the answer - but even if he did, he couldn't give it, because that, according to their hierarchical rules, would be usurping the relevant top group flea's role. Fred instead takes on a role which does not come naturally - but which he has been waiting for the opportunity to try: that of mentor, coach, support, advisor - all very new to Fred, and astounding to the junior flea. This junior flea, it is suggested, has to make up his own mind, and if he makes a mistake, it is being further suggested that he has to trust that "Mr. Fred" would be true to his word and not treat such an outcome as the short sharp end to a promising career.

The junior flea has two sleepless nights and disturbs his home life in deciding what to do. He takes action on day 5 of week 1 - and partially succeeds in achieving his objectives. Fred arrives as promised at the end of that day (full marks to Fred - he kept a promise), warmly praises junior flea for the successful action - and *then* congratulates him effusively for the failed part, after a very positive discussion on the lessons learned from the mistakes made. The junior flea looks about two feet taller.

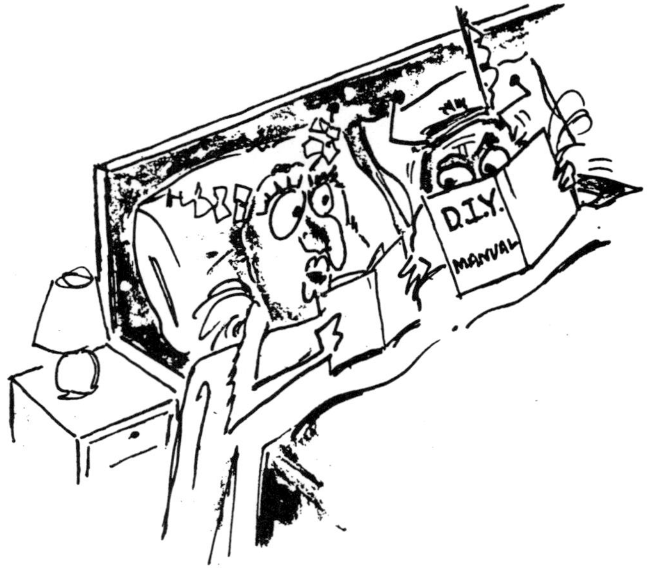

FOR GOODNESS SAKE,
CALM DOWN SIDNEY!

Week 2: Fred walks around for most of this week (with his top group away, the people who trap him in his office are absent). The grapevine has obviously been working overtime, as lots of junior fleas bring their World War III problems to him, discuss them without expecting solutions, go off and take their own actions, come back to Fred and learn from both their successes and failures. They all start looking about two feet taller.

This was cultural change in action. Fred knew he was drawing on a set of values quite different from the old 'fleas in boxes' ones, and living them through the way he was behaving. It was proof that just saying the words is not enough.

Not all of the issues they face are tackled immediately. "Prioritisation" creeps into the language, as does evaluation, risk analysis, and process skills. Many issues are identified and parked as those which the top group fleas should address when they return, all of which have such labels as longer term or strategic.

By the end of week 2, operations are running smoother than ever. There are fewer and fewer fires to put out, the reverse of what would have been predicted with the top group away.

Flea-in-the-box Jack, one of the more annoying and frustrating of fleas - frequently making dramatic jumps from his box in order, apparently, to escape, despite being firmly fixed in it. A flea that is going nowhere until his obvious developmental needs are satisfied.

Week 3: was even more interesting. Firstly, the top group had asked for a meeting with Fred on Day One, and were going to be back on-site for the rest of the week.

At the meeting, Fred asked what they wanted - they had called it, not Fred. The top group said they had some ideas they wanted to "kick around" with Fred. "Are these recommendations?" he asked. No, they said, we just want to see if we are on the right lines. Fred lets them talk for long enough to know that their ideas were on the extreme side of zany. Despite this, he reminded them that the deal was that he would not be involved and would thus make no comment. They went away empty-handed - the megalomaniac much against his better (/trained) nature would give no guidance to his sycophants.

As week 3 wore on (it was less exciting for Fred than weeks 1 and 2 - his top group's presence largely forced him back into his conning tower), Fred became aware that there was friction around, between some of the top group fleas and their junior fleas. Fred said nothing: he couldn't at this point help the junior fleas explain that being given

freedom in a supportive environment was good for everyone.

Week 4: started with Fred seeing Ben, a routine progress meeting except for the hidden agenda of "the plan".

Ben, Fred knew, had had his spies out, and he had not liked what he had heard. Junior fleas in Fred's area seemed to have been taking the law into their own hands, on the back of one major rule having been broken which was that no more than half the top group of fleas were allowed off site at any one time. "Was this the start of anarchy?" Ben enquires, in not too many words? Fred had to do some fast talking especially reminding Ben of his "deal" on the plan Stage 1: to give, effectively, 10 weeks of "space" and that this was only week 4. Ben asked Fred how the plan was progressing - and despite Fred's worst and private thoughts of the apparent chaos the process was in at the moment, he was able to satisfy Ben. He actually only came out of the meeting unscathed because operationally results were currently good and improving.

Week 4 was also interesting because with the top group away again, the junior fleas had reverted to what they had obviously enjoyed during week 1 and 2 - taking action, seeking Fred's advice when they felt it necessary and at all times making sure Fred knew what they were doing. Fred had impressed upon them that he didn't like surprises.

MUST GET DOWN THERE AND ASK THEM WHAT THEY'RE DOING !

Week 5: saw the top group fleas once more trying to draw Fred into the planning process and once more failing.

Fred by this time was becoming quite alarmed - the ideas they were coming up with, as far as he could gather, were still zany and five weeks of the eight had now gone.

It was Fred's turn for sleepless nights - but there's no gain without pain.

Week 6: was different. His top group were on site for a couple of days,but despite Fred's usual, and to date successful attempts to keep informally in touch with what the top group were up to (only because Fred was curious, you understand), now he was meeting a studious and obviously concerted wall of silence. What was going on? - more sleepless nights.

He wondered what genie he had let out of the bottle; where this big (and definitely potentially career-limiting) experiment was taking him. What is all this nonsense about taking risks with people, developing them, giving them the space, letting them out of their boxes, trusting them?

Week 7: came, and all that happened of significance was that the top group asked him to put in his diary the date they wished to present their recommendations in the next week - the last week - week 8. The venue was to be a hotel, miles away.

Week 8: the great day came in the distant hotel. Fred's top group fleas seemed relaxed, purposeful and somehow smug, whilst he, Fred, felt as though he'd been through a mangle.

Strange, he mused, because he had had less and less to do over the last two to three weeks - the junior fleas needing reducing support from Fred in their short-term day to day activities, and the top group fleas hardly speaking to him. His comfortable "action-man" routine had been shattered - that of course was it. This, combined with the fact that with everything going on around him, he hadn't had the

inclination to think about what his real work was for being effective - rather than just being active - in his job.

His thoughts were interrupted by the nominated top group flea member announcing that *it, the team*, would like to present *its* recommendations for Fred's Business Plan. It would take about 30 minutes using flip charts, and *the team* would then be pleased to discuss any issues, and points of clarification, before asking Fred for his reaction.

One by one, several of the top group fleas made their contribution to the presentation. Two things struck Fred about the way the presentation was handled.

Firstly, all of them kept referring to *the team*: how they had enjoyed being part of a peer group, had contributed openly, had found great satisfaction in supporting and helping each other and had become totally committed to the task in hand and its outcome, sometimes at the expense of their individual predilections.

Secondly, and reinforcing the first point, the presenters appeared to have been chosen to contribute to the presentation on their ability to do so, not, as it were, on an ex officio basis.

Strange behaviour indeed.

It was as if they had left their normal individual flea boxes outside the room, and had all jumped into a bigger one together.

His surprise at how the presentation was handled was nothing compared with the content of it.

EXECUTIVE TOILET
5 YEAR PLAN

6. Creative Fleas

The top group (team?) fleas explained that they had translated Fred's 'no constraints' phrase into 'Greenfield Thinking', that is assuming nothing existed. From this starting point, they had 'brainstormed' all of the issues they could possibly think of, and then brainstormed all of the ways they could tackle each issue. From this, they had made choices to create their 'idealised world of Fred'. They explained that this had taken them a lot of time. This idealised world was in many respects unrealistic - zany even - but they explained they had realised that unless they created this idealised world first before 'polluting' it with reality, the inevitable and precious pearls of wisdom that they knew existed in the idealised world would not have been uncovered.

Their next step had been to compare the real world with the idealised, and impose on the idealised only as much of reality as they felt they had to. In that way, they believed they had produced a plan which was closer to the idealised one than if they had started from the other end - the real world - which would have meant seeing how they could, piecemeal, improve on its imperfections.

The plan they unfolded in front of Fred, devised through this Greenfield Process as they called it,

proved beyond doubt to Fred the veracity of the approach they had taken.

The plan contained elements which were so novel, so creative, that Fred could hardly believe that he was listening to his own ordinary to-date-sycophantic fleas. Not only that, their test of 'realistic' for instance had been translated into 'able to meet and beat the financial returns expected in Attila's Empire'. Thus they had selected their *own* constraints within which to work, at the point of *their* choosing - how right Fred had been not to set them any himself!

The sweep of the plan was breathtaking - they had left no stone unturned. It exposed everything to change - physical layouts, operational and information technologies, organisational design, site amenities, pay systems, culture, management style, communications - the list read like a management textbook.

They had not produced detailed solutions on everything but despite this, they were confident of the financial robustness of the plan overall. They explained that the lack of detailed solutions was not because they had not had enough time, although that was certainly the case. It was because they did not know all of the answers (he hadn't heard them admit that before!). They wanted the plan to be implemented, and that integral to its implementation should be its refinement and

development - a principle of "continuous reappraisal and improvement" was extolled. They also wanted cascading involvement down through the organisation, from themselves through the junior fleas to the Indian fleas.

That way two things would happen: all of the ideas of all of the many fleas in Fred's empire would be tapped, and ownership of the plan would spread.

The top group finished their presentation. Would Fred like to comment?

Fred was lost for words. He couldn't think of a single addition or criticism to make of any significance. In any case, he was reeling from the sheer impact of the presentation.

He felt humiliated: here he was, megalomaniac Fred, listening to his sycophants present a plan which was far superior to anything he could have devised. And it wasn't as if there was anything approaching an Einstein amongst them!

The only question he could think of was "How on earth do you think we (note "we") can possibly sell the plan to Ben?".

Well, it wasn't the only question: he started to imagine what would happen if the creative energies of all of his fleas - not just his top group - were channelled and mobilised. They could beat the world!

7. The GreenFlea Plan

Fred divulged for the first time to his top group fleas that he had to present to Ben a Business Plan in two weeks time, and that of course *their* plan had to be the basis. There was no way he, Fred, could possibly think of anything better - indeed, he thanked them for having given him a *vision* of where his part of the organisation could be three years hence.

They enthusiastically responded to Fred's expressed wish for them to be fully involved from now on in helping Fred to run his part of Attila's empire. He wanted them to be a *team* with him as their *leader*, and their first task was to decide how they as a team would *sell their* plan, first to Ben.

At the subsequent off-site meeting the next day (they weren't worried about being off-site now - the junior fleas were coping very well with the day-to-day operations), they shared their new-found knowledge: Fred's during devolution, the Quality Circles experiment, and sending the group away; and the group's from the peer group environment generated during the creation of the plan - the Greenfield process and so on.

They vowed never again to leave any team meeting until, as the final item, they explicitly exchanged what they had learned since the last session. That

way, the learning process would become more systematic and thus more effective, and they could continuously improve individually and as a team, for instance through learning more about each other's strengths and drawing on them. Almost as a bonus - such an understanding would be a basis for individual and team development. Training for example would for them from now on have a targeted organisational purpose.

Having decided in the round the team *processes* they were going to use, they turned their attention to the *task* in hand: selling their plan to Ben.

They analysed his needs - his customer needs; identified what in their plan could meet them - these were the items they would bring to the fore; they identified what would threaten him (there was *lots* of that!) - they would articulate as best they could how to contain such threats. They branded the plan the GreenFlea Plan; they decided how best to make the presentation - flip charts and diagrams (with costs coming down, turnover going up etc!); they decided who would be the salesmen, choosing carefully who they thought Ben warmed to most; they allocated individuals with sections of the presentation to prepare; and agreed to meet the next week for the dress rehearsal, timed for only 3 days before they were due 'on parade' in front of Ben.

Finally, they shared the learning experiences of the day.

The major one was that of *ownership*, whether of ideas or of physical things. Here they were, the 'top group fleas' (i.e. Fred's team less Fred) absolutely determined that *their* plan was not going to fail because it *was* theirs. They had put Fred on the line - he hadn't better fail to deliver *their* plan as their 'super salesman'. By comparison, all previous plans in which they had been involved had been handed down by Fred as the tablet of stone from above - and they had never felt committed to them. Compliance had been the 'name of the game', taking no risks, keeping in flea-box comfort zones and out of danger.

This analysis suggested that there is no neutral ground with regard to ownership; the 'not invented here' syndrome being a good example. You either championed an idea, or you rejected it.

So their focus with Ben was for him to take ownership of their plan.

Indeed the focus of any process they initiated from now on would be spreading ownership.

UM! NOT MINE, NOT THEIRS,
BUT OURS EH!

THE SWAT SQUAD

8. Attila is Swatted

The day before the GreenFlea Plan was to be presented, Ben cancelled the meeting.

Fred and his team were devastated, fearing that their product would never see the light of day. They imagined some devious manipulation of them by Ben: that would not be out of character for "Corporate Flea".

To add to their anxiety all managerial fleas were summoned to a special meeting to hear a major announcement.

The grapevine went into overdrive as usual in such situations, and as usual got it wrong.

The announcement in fact started with the news that Attila had left.

Now that *was* a good reason for Ben to have cancelled their GreenFlea meeting: Attila had been swatted! It was obvious, from the way this termination was described, that the real reasons for him being swatted - and indeed, who had wielded the flea swat - would never emerge, but none the less it was a fact that he had been swatted.

M5
OUTER
MONGOLIA

The announcement went on to say that a new, and lady, flea called Fiona, was to take his place and that she would be arriving on the following Monday.

Well ..... all the fleas immediately started jumping about in quite an agitated manner - this was very unsettling news. Attila had been the one over the years who had ultimately decided all the rules for how each and every one of the fleas' individual boxes - their comfort zones - had been prescribed. Thus, their concern was how the change would affect their boxes - boxes that had been comfortable and safe havens, within which they felt insulated from threats. Without Attila around, Fiona could rattle them, reshape them - even dispose of them.

Fred's reaction was quite different. With such a change of leadership at the top, he saw the potential for overcoming all constraints, both real and imagined. Indeed, he saw such a change as being the *only* way for this to be even a possibility: an 'agent of change' more powerful, arguably, than any.

He looked forward to Fiona's arrival with eager anticipation.

Pondering on the needs and expectations of the new internal customer ....

9. Fiona, Queen Flea

On arrival, Fiona immediately turned all the fleas' worlds upside down. She walked around: she was visible. She talked a new language - teamwork, support, openness. She listened. She even had lunch - chips and egg, for goodness sake - on her first day in the works canteen, the lowest pig-flea trough in the hierarchy of six eating facilities (six - such a number often amazed even the most corporate of fleas - the inventive ingenuity of status-driven fleas knows no bounds).

Her third day was devoted to addressing the management fleas. The themes of her presentation stunned the audience:

- She had a long range view of the organisation described in unfamiliar words such as "vision, excellence, and values".

- She asserted that the organisation's fleas were the only long-term source of competitive advantage

- The central role of management fleas was to lead, not to control, the efforts of others; to support them in optimising their individual and collective contributions. Words such as "empowerment" and "ownership" slipped gracefully from her tongue.

- The focus of the organisation should be centred on satisfying customers, not on sycophant fleas pleasing megalomaniac fleas (this was Fred's interpretation of what she actually said).

- Risk-taking was to become a core value, and the inevitable mistakes would be the seed-corn for experiential learning and continuous improvement.

- Systems, procedures and policy frameworks would be rewritten towards outputs - results - not as historically on inputs and processes; and for which individuals and teams should be given the utmost freedom to achieve within sensible frameworks.

To support these themes, she asked the assembled management fleas to address what to most was a devastating issue: if you are not satisfied with the way your subordinate fleas are behaving (and in two short days since she had arrived, she had obviously established that there was a large degree of dissatisfaction) have you asked yourselves these questions: Why do they behave the way they do? Why do they behave differently from you? Is it because you think they are inherently different? Or is it because of what is in place around them - the systems, the policies, the procedures we generate - the training we provide - the information we allow (or rather do not allow) access to - the communication processes we adopt - the internal environment we create - the role models (particularly ourselves) we (perhaps by inference only) ask them to copy?

The message was stark and simple: "we" are the recipients of the behaviours we deserve from "them", behaviours which are very largely generated by management actions and decisions, so management has only itself to blame for the results.

She finished up by modestly - and truthfully - admitting that whilst she had a clear personal philosophy, she did not have any plans or solutions to impose. She did want to move the organisation forward, and promised that she would listen to ideas openly and constructively on how that could be done from those who knew the business best: the fleas within it.

On returning to their boxes, 'bewilderment' describes the general feeling of the vast majority of fleas in response to the presentation. It was as if they were sitting immobile in their boxes, wondering how they should now jump, peering around to see if their boxes were still there and if so - did those boxes now have any relevance?

Within only a few short hours the fleas could be observed jumping around just as before. But they would - wouldn't they? Remember Devolution? Attila's training, his conditioning of them, was deep-seated in their flea brains. It would take a lot more than a pronouncement to change all that.

Naturally, all Fred could see was the opportunity to capitalise on all the work he and his own fleas had done.

YOU WILL FORGET ATTILA!
YOU WILL FORGET ATTILA!

BLESS
THIS
LOUSE

10. Fred's Fleas Prepare

Events moved quickly.

The rearranged presentation of GreenFlea Plan to Ben went well. He reacted enthusiastically to it, and arranged that a repeat of the presentation be made to Fiona and her executive team (yes, Ben used that word).

This second presentation went even better (having already had what amounted to a dress rehearsal with Ben), with Fred and his fleas all contributing to a magnificent team performance selling their product - the GreenFlea Plan.

Some of the more notable points of the event were:

- The process they had used, centred around: identifying 'where do we want to be (using Greenfield Thinking, of course)?'; 'where are we now?'; analysing the gap between the two; and describing the implementation steps to close the gap.

- The holistic manner in which they had applied this process, describing the desired relationships with all the stakeholders who had an interest in their business, and how all of the resources at their disposal within the business could be

marshalled and focused in a prioritised way to achieve the clear organisational goals included in their plan.

- And most importantly, that despite what they felt was the thorough approach they were describing to change the organisation, it most certainly could and must be improved by involving more fleas before implementation was started in earnest, and indeed that implementation must be centred around all of the fleas within the organisation taking ownership of the changes in a progressive way over time.

It was Fred himself who picked upon this last point to conclude the presentation. In what had by now become a routine process for Fred and his team, prior to the presentation they had analysed the expectations of their newest customer - Fiona - and so the peroration which Fred delivered was targeted to hit her quite obvious 'people: behavioural' hot spots thus:

"There are many within the organisation who believe that the majority of our fleas have little to offer outside very limited boundaries. The greatest proportion who hold this view are senior and middle management fleas - those who perceive that they have the most to lose if the status quo is changed. They do not yet appreciate that if we ever create an

environment where we unleash the talents of all of our fleas and channel their energies to fulfil our chosen mission, we will be world-beaters, and so everyone can gain.

For those who hold such views, let them consider some examples from our current situation:

- If we give them a pig trough to eat from, should we be surprised if they behave like pigs?

- If they see management fleas fighting for the biggest and most prestigious offices, carpets, cars and parking spaces, should we be surprised if they themselves become motivated by (often counterproductive) status symbols?

- If we lavish training on ourselves alone, should we be surprised if they appear (and indeed will be) unskilled and ignorant, able to do only wholly prescribed tasks?

- If we do not inform them of business realities, should we be surprised if they do not react sensibly to them?

- If we only ever communicate to them in a serious way when there is bad news to tell them, should we be surprised if they appear not to be interested in company affairs?

- If they have 'second class' terms and conditions of employment, should we be surprised if they act as if they are 'second class citizens'?

- If we treat them as if they have no brains, should we be surprised if they conduct themselves as if they were brainless?

- If we constantly impose solutions without their involvement in arriving at them, should we be surprised if they often react against them?

- If we say one thing and do another, should we be surprised if they are confused and mistrustful?

- If we act like megalomaniacs, should we be surprised if they behave like sycophants."

Fiona and her team approved the plan.

Not only that, they all supported the idea, proposed by Ben, that this plan, which would transform Fred's areas of activities, would be used as a model from which others could learn, so that similar plans could be implemented as soon as possible across the whole of the organisation.

Fred was told to 'get jumping'.

At his first Implementation Team meeting, the *first* item on the agenda was for him and his team to share their learning experiences from the whirlwind of events.

Their analysis concluded that:

- The catalyst was Fiona. The GreenFlea Plan was exactly in line with her stated philosophy.

- Ben's corporate survival instincts - not any latent deep-seated beliefs - had led him to be seen to be championing the plan. It now represented the vehicle for him to ingratiate himself with Fiona, and thus to continue to survive.

He could and would boast that it was *his* clever little fleas who, with *his* encouragement, had hatched this innovative approach.

- They should not get depressed about this conclusion - quite the opposite. It merely meant that the means by which they would manage Ben had changed. They would ensure that he was kept on side, in exchange for which they would expect him to keep all of his peer fleas off their backs when the inevitable opportunities appeared to swat Fred and his team. The major changes they were about to unleash would be very threatening to all the fleas in all their old boxes, boxes they would give up with the greatest reluctance.

Fred and his fleas then drew breath, thinking about the workload ahead of them .....

NEW HORIZONS

Section III

Metamorphosis

FLEA
MARKET
SECOND
HAND
FLEA
BOXES
SALE

1. The Fleas Fly

Fred and his fleas successfully implemented their plan - *but that's* **another** *story.*

o-O-o-O-o-O-o-O-o

Of course, Fred was not *really* a flea. He was a manager, who *used* to behave like so many others, jumping around in their boxes - their comfort zones - never straying into the neutral zones around them, let alone taking serious risks by venturing into the danger zones.

Fred had had the courage to do so, and thus to go through a learning experience, a transformation - a metamorphosis. He grew into a leader, seemingly able to fly, to soar to new heights, to broaden his vision of what he, *and* others, *and* his organisation were capable of.

The quintessence of his transformation was that he inspired the other fleas around him to transform themselves, within the supportive environment which he fostered.

He grew by growing them.

Simple, really.

YES I CAN REMEMBER 50 YEARS AGO WHEN THE WHOLE OF THIS SITE WAS COVERED IN LITTLE BOXES AS FAR AS THE EYE COULD SEE!

About the author:

David L. Cox

David is an International Business Consultant, assisting organisations around the world to manage strategic and cultural change.

He has developed a considerable reputation for facilitating workshops with senior executives and helping with subsequent corporate renewal programmes such as those with National Grid, Hongkong Telecom, The Cabinet Office, PIVOT (Australia) and Chevron Shipping (San Francisco).

His consultancy activities are supplemented by Board Membership of several companies, and by lecturing as an occasional member of faculty at numerous business schools in the UK including Cranfield School of Management, Ashridge Management College, Henley the Management College, London Business School, Templeton College Oxford, and The Judge Institute of Management Studies, Cambridge.

He started his career in 1963 when he joined Allied Breweries with an Honours Degree in Biochemistry. After a series of appointments in Allied Breweries in Birmingham, Burton and Warrington, he became Managing Director of the Ind Coope Burton Brewery in 1982 and in 1986 he was appointed a Main Board Director of Allied. He held these positions until April 1988, during which time he led a major structural reorganisation. His book *Exploiting Change, By GABB and By GIBB* is an account of this project, an account which has since been extended into a full range of distance learning training materials.

For further information:

Fax: 0543 481815 International +44 543 481815

About the cartoonist:

Bryan Jones

A Member of the
Cartoonists' Club of Great Britain

Bryan first became associated with David Cox at Allied Breweries and has worked on previous projects including David's first book *Exploiting Change.*

Bryan is a member of the Cartoonists' Club of Great Britain and is currently a freelance cartoonist in the Midlands area of the UK producing work for the press, training videos and company magazines.

For further information:

Telephone: 0283 66935 International +44 283 66935

jos

Bryan couldn't stop drawing .....

THERE'S DEFINITELY NOTHING BETWEEN HERE AND THE OTHER ONE FRED.

American-Flea

Euro - Flea

TO LET
WRITE
BOX 22

WHEN I SAY JUMP – I MEAN JUMP!

Guy Fawkes – Flea